Uncovering the Resilient Core

Uncoverir   meth-
odology   f the
therapeu   th its
psychody   egins
with char   understanding   ssism,
including   . The
applied n   s well
as progre   tic listening sk   tment
examples   used
in your o   edge.
com/978   ng the
learning

Patricia   r with
over thir   sycho-
logical S   Wayne
Institute

Jack Da   er, and
consulta   Karen
Horney   as lectured na   communication, and intergenerational effects of trauma.

Patricia Gianotti and Jack Danielian can be contacted through their website,
www.treatingnarcissism.com.

"Danielian and Gianotti have done it again! —yet another magnificent volume that seamlessly integrates theory and practice as it addresses both the science and the art of an in-depth psychotherapeutic process. Exquisitely penned by two master clinicians, this second opus is an elegant and sophisticated Workbook that explores, in great detail, both the nuances and the complexities of the moment-to-moment encounter between patient and therapist. Culled from their decades of immersion in the study, the practice, and the teaching of a psychotherapeutic approach that is a synergistic blend of elements that are at once self-psychological, existential, humanistic, empathic, present-focused, relational, attachment-based, systemic, Horneyian, and spiritual, at the end of the day the paradigm they espouse—exemplified by their Four Quadrant Model—can probably best be described as either "Danottian" or "Gianelian."

But however we might describe their theoretical stance, what shines through on every page of this brilliantly conceived and beautifully orchestrated manual is their non-pathologizing optimism and profound belief in the patient's innate resilience and capacity to self-repair. Against a therapeutic backdrop of reliability, attunement, and profound respect, patient and therapist work at their intimate edge to help the patient relinquish self-sabotaging but once adaptive narcissistic defenses mobilized to compensate for feelings of vulnerability and shame; heal the psychic split between the defensively dissociated parts of the patient's character structure and the parts that are more spontaneous, heartfelt, and healthy; emancipate the patient's resilient core; and facilitate the emergence of an integrated, consolidated, authentic self.

No offense intended to any of my other esteemed colleagues (or to myself for that matter), but were I to be alone on a desert island with only one book, this is the book that I would want to have—and I would read and reread it many times over, each time gleaning something new and inspirational. Quite frankly, I wish I had written this extraordinary book. It is so beautifully and sensitively written and explores with such finesse all the fine points and subtleties of the therapeutic relationship that it should be required reading for therapists of all levels. And the material is so rich and layered that I found myself wanting to peruse only a few pages at a time so that I could process and integrate the wealth of information contained on each page and savor every pearl of wisdom contained therein.

This lovingly and generously crafted masterpiece is a tome that I will long cherish. But I will not keep it on my bookshelf; I will want it in plain sight on my desk by my side—to guide me and to inspire me."—**Martha Stark, MD**, faculty, Harvard Medical School; co-director, Center for Psychoanalytic Studies; author, award-winning *Modes of Therapeutic Action* and five other books on psychoanalytic theory and practice

Uncovering the Resilient Core
A Workbook on the Treatment of Narcissistic Defenses, Shame, and Emerging Authenticity

Patricia Gianotti and Jack Danielian

Routledge
Taylor & Francis Group

NEW YORK AND LONDON

First published 2017
by Routledge
711 Third Avenue, New York, NY 10017

and by Routledge
2 Park Square, Milton Park, Abingdon, Oxon, OX14 4RN

Routledge is an imprint of the Taylor & Francis Group, an informa business

Library of Congress Cataloging-in-Publication Data
Names: Gianotti, Patricia, 1949– author. | Danielian, Jack, 1934– author.
Title: Uncovering the resilient core : a workbook on the treatment of narcissistic defenses, shame, and emerging authenticity / by Patricia Gianotti and Jack Danielian.
Description: New York, NY : Routledge, 2017. Includes bibliographical references and index.
Identifiers: LCCN 2016041450 | ISBN 9781138183278 (hbk. : alk. paper) | ISBN 9781138183285 (pbk. : alk. paper) | ISBN 9781315645926 (eBook)
Subjects: | MESH: Psychological Trauma—therapy | Psychotherapy—methods | Shame | Narcissism | Resilience, Psychological | Professional-Patient Relations
Classification: LCC RC480.5 NLM WM 420 DDC 616.89/14—dc23
LC record available at https://lccn.loc.gov/2016041450

ISBN: 978-1-138-18327-8 (hbk)
ISBN: 978-1-138-18328-5 (pbk)
ISBN: 978-1-315-64592-6 (ebk)

Typeset in Frutiger Light
by Apex CoVantage, LLC

Visit the eResources: www.routledge.com/book/9781138183285

Contents

Figures

Foreword

Not for the faint of heart, the effort to teach or to learn the "craft and spirit" of psychotherapy, as master of such teachings, Joseph Lichtenberg (Lichtenberg, 2005), puts it. The Workbook you hold in your hands, companion to Patricia Gianotti and Jack Danielian's (Danielian and Gianotti, 2012) *Listening with Purpose: Entry Points into Shame and Narcissistic Vulnerability*, combines hands-on practicality for the beginner with the attitudes and spirit a clinician gains only with years of practice. Though it explicitly addresses the beginning therapist in training, note well: beginning and experienced supervisors can find nourishment and focus as well. What makes this book so valuable?

First, dear to my heart, comes the nearly jargon-free language, despite reliance on the best of the psychoanalytic tradition, including recent relational and intersubjective versions, creating accessibility for those schooled in the dominant "evidence-based" models of today. Yes, Gianotti and Danielian write of transference and dissociation, but with enough examples, explanations, and stories to make them come to life in all their complexity. Indeed the book seems deceptively simple until the reader realizes how much complexity the student therapist is being taught to hold without reductionism. The authors hold and guide the student reader, as well as beginning supervisors, so that their readers will be able to hold the complexity of traumatic experience, shame, and relational process. Challenges and clinician self-doubt will inevitably arrive, they warn. At the same time, their questions both open the reader's mind and express the expectancy—"forecast," they would say—for the beginning therapist's capacity for clinical thinking and relating.

A second great gift, in my view, comes in their linking, as does Judith Lewis Herman (Herman, 2011), shame with trauma—actually with every emotional human trouble, often called pathology. Their focus on the centrality of shame in clinical work with every form of trauma, especially in extreme dissociation (work always requiring supervision!) incorporates the best insights of the many psychoanalytic "shameniks," among whom I count myself, as well as, implicitly those of Sandra Buechler on shame in clinical training (Buechler, 2008). These authors teach trainees to pick up subtle clues to shame, as well as extreme and suicidal self-hatred. I can only wish I had had them as teachers many years ago.

Finally, subtle but still radical and most welcome of all, I find a turn toward what I have described as a "hermeneutics of trust" (Orange, 2011), an attitude ascribing to the other good intentions. The patients are doing their best to survive a bad situation, to cope with the hand—sometimes extremely bad—that they were dealt, by family, history, circumstances. Staying as close as possible to the patients' experience, treating "defenses" (the old language) as means of survival to live another day, these authors teach new therapists not only methods, but methods that express attitudes of hospitality and care. What we may need to sustain and nourish these attitudes for many years, I have recently described as the development of an internal chorus (Orange, 2016). To become a clinician, day by day, hour by hour, who treats the other as a human being of infinite value, invested in the restoration of hope and dignity, starts with this book.

Donna M. Orange, PhD, PsyD
Assistant Clinical Professor (Adjunct) and Consultant/Supervisor
New York University Post-Doctoral Program in Psychotherapy and
Psychoanalysis

References

Buechler, S. (2008). The Legacies of Shaming Psychoanalytic Candidates. *Contemp: Psychoanal, 44*, 56–64.

Danielian, J., & Gianotti, P. (2012). *Listening with Purpose: Entry Points into Shame and Narcissistic Vulnerability.* New York: Jason Aronson.

Herman, J. (2011). Posttraumatic Stress Disorder as a Shame Disorder. In R. Dearing & J. Tangney, eds., *Shame in the Therapy Hour* (pp. 261–276). Washington, DC: American Psychological Association.

Lichtenberg, J. D. (2005). *Craft and Spirit: A Guide to the Exploratory Psychotherapies.* Hillsdale, NJ: The Analytic Press.

Orange, D. M. (2011). *The Suffering Stranger: Hermeneutics for Everyday Clinical Practice.* New York: Routledge/Taylor & Francis Group.

Orange, D. M. (2016). *Nourishing the Inner Life of Clinicians and Humanitarians: The Ethical Turn in Psychoanalysis.* London and New York: Routledge.

Acknowledgments

The effort it takes to complete a book would often appear daunting, if it were not for the support and wise counsel of colleagues and contemporaries, both past and present, who provide their expertise and guidance along the way. We begin by paying tribute to those clinicians and thinkers that came before us, each of whom have laid stepping stones of theoretical insight that add to the ever-evolving landscape of clinical practice.

We owe much to many, but we owe the most to our patients. We are especially grateful for their courage and perseverance in travelling often difficult terrains to find their true selves. It is through their relational connection to us that we are able to discover the never-ending complexities and nuances of growth as practitioners. It is by joining them in the present moment-to-moment that we were able to listen more deeply, feel more deeply, and hopefully refine our capabilities in our effort to embrace their unique narratives.

There are numerous individuals who helped make the completion of this book possible. We want to especially thank Donna M. Orange for graciously writing the Foreword to our book. Thanks also go to Paul Wachtel, Martha Stark, and Jon Mills for their endorsements of our work. We also want to give special thanks to Dr. Kenneth Cohen and Dr. Davelyn Vidrine, colleagues who generously gave us their input around the use of language, content, and theoretical constructs. Additional thanks are extended to Dr. Davelyn Vidrine for her willingness to be videotaped and to speak extemporaneously on the power of the Four Quadrant Model as applied to her own clinical work. Other colleagues, Donna Knudsen and LR Berger, have been instrumental in offering their wise counsel around alternative treatment approaches to shame and trauma as they can be incorporated into more traditional psychodynamic frameworks.

The numerous videos that are included in this training manual were created with the help of a host of local actors and production assistants. We begin by thanking our video editors, Bill Humphreys of Portsmouth Public Media TV, and his intern assistants, Chad Cordner, Colin McCarthy, and Kevin Russell. We also give thanks to Jonathan Niketh, editor, technical wizard, and go-to person for all questions that required technical support.

We wish to credit the following actors: Genevieve Aichele, from New Hampshire Theater Project, Blair Hundertmark, Bill Humphreys, Jasmin Hunter, Todd Hunter, CJ Lewis, Colleen Madden, Sarah McPhee, Lauren Monteleon, Jonathan Niketh, Linette Roungchun, Dominque Salvachion, Danny Dwaine Wells, and Constance Witman. Although the videos used in this Workbook were remarkable excerpts from actual treatment sessions or condensed syntheses of several sessions, all scenes were played by actors.

We extend *deep* appreciation to our editor at Routledge, Elizabeth Graber. Her knowledge, encouragement, and wise perspective directed our progress every step of the way. Thank you, Elizabeth, for your editorial suggestions, your patience, and your wonderful sense of humor.

We wish to acknowledge and give thanks to Ani Danielian Huang for her generous help in proofreading and copyediting the manuscript and to Emiko Danielian who provided her creative graphic expertise to the figures and graphs included in the text. A special thanks goes to Pamela Wallace, for allowing us to use her essay as the Epilogue of our book. Finally, we give our deepest thanks to Stephen Gianotti and Hasmig Danielian for their loving support and patience around this endeavor.

Introduction

For too many years in mental health work, shame and trauma have been our therapeutic orphans. This has dramatically reduced our capacity to understand and treat an entire range of patients. The reasons have been myriad but chief among them has been a model of dynamic thinking rooted in traditional instinct theory. Guilt and repression were seen as the principal building blocks of psychopathology, while character structure was deemed to be peripheral to any depth of investigation. As a result, shame and trauma became relegated to secondary status and were seen as perhaps not relevant at all to successful dynamic treatment.

And then the world caught up with us. More and more of our patients appear to be suffering from narcissistic injury, ruptures of attunement, trauma, and abuse. Although most clinicians in contemporary practice now believe that human development can only be understood from a relational perspective, the study of shame and trauma is still a relatively young field. We similarly believe that when ideas of attachment and relationality are used as the focal point in clinical thinking, we become open to a more experience-near treatment approach. Focusing on the symptoms historically marginalized in our field (shame, self-hate, dissociation, and narcissism), crises of identity come more directly into the foreground of both listening and treatment.

Adequate processing of shame and shame derivatives involves no clinical short cuts. The defensive character formations formed in the wake of disconnected or dissociated shame can be formidable and require delicate clinical handling. As Harry Stack Sullivan (1953) reminds us, "All of us are much more human than otherwise." In response to this challenge, the Workbook we have created is clearly devoted to a deeper and more intimate appreciation of the personal cost of these disorders, with major attention to the moment-to-moment listening capacity so important to their effective treatment.

Our work follows advances in the field of shame made by many relationally attuned thinkers such as Ainsworth, Bowlby, Broucek, Lewis, Herman, Morrison, Nathanson, Orange, Stern, Stark, Stolorow, and Wachtel. Earlier still, courageous writers such as Horney and Ferenczi opened up the field of trauma, often at great cost to themselves, but with great benefit to the mental health field.

Clinical studies on shame continue today as we speak. Margaret Crastnopol (2015) has helpfully expanded the continuum of trauma to include micro-trauma that can develop over the course of childhood into a damaging "cumulative psychic injury." In her words, "these micro-traumatic situations . . . can be hidden in plain sight [and] since these injurious moments occur within relationships that are otherwise felt to be valuable, the individual may be motivated to ignore them in service of not rocking the relational boat" (p. 3).

Delving further into the treatment of these painful and sometimes elusive disorders, Patricia A. DeYoung (2015) captures the destructive nature of intense shame when she says that shame makes people feel "blank, 'vaporized,' or incoherent, even to themselves. In moments of feeling humiliated, they can't speak, or even think . . . [t]he threat of psychological annihilation is mirrored by their wish to sink through the floor or to disappear, in some way just to cease to exist" (p. 19).

The field of shame is making progress. Neurobiological research in the areas of trauma and relational attachment styles, particularly the work of Allan Schore, Daniel Siegel, Leigh McCullough Vaillant, and Diana Fosha, have provided spring-boards for new thinking and dialogue across therapeutic disciplines. Toward that end, our Workbook directly proceeds to tackle the imperative of training thera-pists in the depth treatment of shame and trauma. Yet, to date, we have seen very little hands-on training in how to track shame moment-to-moment in a sustained way, and how to track micro-dissociations triggered by shame within the treatment hour. Theory is only as good as the training it inspires.

The brain processes a range of conscious and non-conscious material, what we recognize about ourselves and what we verbally do not recognize about ourselves. The range of conscious and non-conscious material processed by the brain is the very material we deal with in our systemic training, namely the sys-temic connections between the cognitive, the behavioral, and the affective. In a conflicted state of mind, information cannot be readily processed and remains in a "frozen" state. Our approach, geared to the phenomenological *here and now*, is carefully designed to track these frozen memories in their dissociated state,

In recent years, significant progress has been made in empirically validating the particular value of longer-term therapies (Bateman and Fonagy, 2008; Cur-tis, 2014; Fonagy, et al., 2015; Sheldon, 2010). Especially through the fastidious work of Fonagy, et al., the Tavistock Institute of London, England has pub-lished in *World Psychiatry* (2015) a randomized and very well-controlled study demonstrating the clear efficiency of longer-term treatment (eighteen months) for patients suffering from chronic depression. Forty-four percent of patients with major depressive symptoms no longer had these symptoms after treatment ended, while only ten percent of the shorter-term patients responded. Further-more, after three and a half years of observation, the longer-term patients had a forty percent higher rate of partial remission than the shorter-term patients. Tavistock concludes that longer-term therapy has clear beneficial results not only in terms of symptom relief and personal growth but for "a lasting gain in resilience."

Healing from past trauma occurs when the therapist can sustain a secure envi-ronment. A secure therapeutic environment helps to promote the delicate vibra-tions of unconscious or blocked affect, created from past relational ruptures, to be experienced in the present moment. To be sure, it is a present-focused, relational approach that is informed moment-to-moment by a patient's evolved attachment style and the moment-to-moment intrapsychic systems compulsively fueling that style.

Simultaneously tracking the interpersonal and intrapsychic components in real time offers us our best opportunity to identify the ever-present and precious potential for growth in each of our patients. As the process occurs, self-realizing builds on itself and is better able to sustain its gains through future challenges, including unconscious attempts at psychic self-sabotage. Witnessing this process of psychological change over and over again cannot but be a building block of hope for both the involved patient and the involved therapist.

As suggested, opposing mechanisms inevitably come into play to self-protect the patient's increasing sense of exposure and dread. An entire range of dissociations may be involved that bypasses the attention of the patient and frequently the therapist as well. Moving closer and closer to the more intensive tracking highlighted in this Workbook brings us ever closer to the workings of inner health. This seeming paradox is actually the *gateway* to successful treatment.

In our experience, the gateway to a patient's inner health is best accessed through what has been called in recent writings "the framework of resilience." If we embrace the notion that the human spirit contains an innate capacity for resilience, *how we listen* to our patient narratives may create subtle shifts in *what we listen* for. When the dialogic exchange becomes influenced by our inner belief in a patient's resilience, this sense of optimism can fundamentally change the field and ground of how we view both our patients and our work as clinicians.

However, a caveat is indicated. Under conditions that violate our sense of self and basic safety, none of us are immune to unconsciously creating a false sense of security in an attempt to distance from feelings of anxiety and vulnerability. Yet, this is a spurious security, one that often co-opts and hijacks our best resources, resources such as curiosity, proactivity, and the evolving emergence of our unique, authentic selves. Knowing this, we need to take caution in understanding how easily, under the right conditions, we can succumb to over-idealizing our best assets in an attempt to mold them to externally driven expectations and standards. But we remind ourselves that whatever remains in our reach is that which is in-born within us, not a compulsively created *substitute* of our real selves.

Our innate capacity for resilience allows us to heal. At the same time, it is the over-idealization of that capacity that can convince us that our resilience is boundless, which is to say that we believe we cannot be hurt by pain, loss, or humiliation.

The see-saw confusion between healthy optimism and an over-determined posture of false optimism has plagued both the mental health field and our culture at large for quite some time. At the heart of this confusion is a lack of clarity around the power that shame holds on the human psyche, and what the grip of shame can do to cripple the human spirit. Whereas resilience activates hope in us, shame evokes feelings of dread, discomfort, and a sense of unworthiness. The mention of shame often has a powerful contagion effect that is difficult to escape, making the denial and avoidance of shame all the more intense.

Feelings of shame and unworthiness typically stem from childhood conditions that include varying degrees of abuse and/or neglect. No one is immune to being activated by shame, although shame triggers vary in intensity and scope from individual to individual. The intensity and scope of shame is often relative to the quality of the parent-child bond, whether the attachment was secure, insecure, or disorganized. Insecure attachments are traumatic. Although children quickly learn to adapt and compensate, it is often at the expense of healthy development. And we might add that neuroscientific research now affirms that trauma leaves a long wake in its path, neurologically, emotionally, and relationally.

The long wake of trauma typically manifests in adulthood as narcissistic defenses. These are acquired protective mechanisms that patients develop in an attempt to compensate for shameful feelings of fear or inadequacy. However, these compulsively driven attitudes and behaviors are *unsustainable* over time. Invariably, any defensive mechanism requires more and more effort to maintain because the source of the pain is not yet understood or metabolized. Failed ambitions, the aging process, life's disappointments and losses often result in a patient's increased rigidity in attitudes and beliefs.

When grandiosity, self-sacrifice, or naiveté morph into increasing bitterness and a narrowing of life, a breakthrough of symptoms often emerges. Yet, at any stage of life, the continuing presence of real resilience offers hope and an opportunity for self-reflection, thereby opening doorways of natural curiosity that can lead to a change in perspective. As midwives to the emergence of authenticity, the patient's nascent signs of resilience can lend a vitally important hand in long-term therapeutic discovery and emancipation. Intensive tracking of inner health, as evidenced through a patient's core resilience, will be highlighted throughout this Workbook in numerous case studies and therapeutic vignettes.

In the understudied and still neglected approach to a constructivist treatment of shame, a principal task is for the therapist to gradually and gingerly identify tendrils of health not yet within the patient's grasp. The process of treatment becomes not just dealing with "mechanisms" but emancipating the resilient core of the patient to grow to its fuller capacity. Among many others, victims of shame and trauma become beneficiaries. Clear recognition of the capacity for health and resilience as *in-born* to our nature, and available to all of us, liberates the process of therapeutic healing to be seen as a more humanistic, optimistic, and self-realizing endeavor.

A Note about the Cover of This Book

The photograph used for the cover of this book was taken by Stephen Gianotti (with minimal assistance from his wife, who offered moral support). This image was shot along the coastline of New Castle, NH, at 3:00 in the morning.

Imagine the scene—it was the middle of winter, temperatures below freezing, and it was pitch black outside. There was no moon; no stars were visible to the naked eye. You quite literally could not see the hand in front of your face. Only the lighthouse off Wood Island provided intermittent, brief flashes of light that helped us find our way down to the rocks.

This image was shot with film, before digital cameras had eclipsed the creative art of film photography. Stephen used a medium format Hasselblad camera for this photograph, with an eight-minute exposure. Given the conditions, we did not know what the camera lens would capture. Several shots were taken with shorter exposures—two minutes, three minutes, five minutes—all revealing nothing more than black negatives when we got the film back from the developer. Then, there was the eight-minute exposure. When I saw the image, I reflected on my own thoughts that night while standing there in the freezing darkness, asking myself, "Are we crazy?" But, Stephen was patient. He kept saying, "Just give it a little more time. Just give it a little more time."

Much like the capturing of light through the camera lens, the therapeutic journey takes the time it will take before enough light illuminates what is hidden from view. With our patients, often the process takes more time than they think. Metaphorically speaking, patient and therapist begin in the dark, neither being exactly sure what will be revealed nor where the journey will take them. Gradually, landmarks and solid ground begin to emerge. Trust deepens. The process unfolds.

Over the course of our long careers, we have seen time and again that the therapeutic process can be a powerful tool in the service of healing and growth. Given enough time, and offering the right combination of encouragement, deep listening, and confidence in the resilience of the human spirit, the light of the emerging self generally shines through.

1

Resilience
An Overview and Introduction

Be a provenance of something gathered, a summation of previous intuitions, let your vulnerabilities walking on the cracked, sliding limestone, be this time, not a weakness, but a faculty for understanding what's about to happen.
—David Whyte, excerpt from "The Seven Streams,"
from *River Flow: New and Selected Poems*
©Many Rivers Press, Langley, WA, USA.
Printed with permission from Many Rivers.

David Whyte's poetic words serve as an introduction to this text, an invitation to explore the often complex and variable nuances of the therapeutic process. Our goal for this Workbook is to explore and revisit basic, fundamental principles that answer the question, "What makes for a good psychotherapy experience?" Using a relational paradigm, we might also ask, "What are the essential elements of a therapeutic holding environment? How do we co-create a relational incubator for healing, recovery, and development throughout the life span?"

The process of psychotherapy is much like an invisible current that surfaces and resonates between patient and therapist. Following the various currents or self-states that branch and connect back toward the "real" or authentic self is a process that requires courage and trust, introspection and memory, grieving and letting go, in addition to adjusting expectations of self and other. Attending to these various components of the therapeutic journey ultimately leads to integration and growth. As the title of our book, *Uncovering the Resilient Core*, suggests, we will weave the concept of resilience (itself also an underground river current) throughout the various themes and learning points covered in each chapter.

The textbook understanding of the term "resilience" highlights the concrete physical parameters of resilience, defining it as "the physical property of a material that can return to its original shape or position after deformation that does not exceed its elastic limit." The psychological, medical, or emotional interpretation of resilience refers to it as one's ability to recover from illness, depression,

1

and adversity and the measure of one's strength, toughness, adaptability, hardiness, and the capacity to withstand stress.

Based on the principles of physical science, one could extrapolate that psychotherapy is, in fact, in the *service of* resilience. The fundamental aim of successful psychotherapy is to help the patient regain his or her natural ability to return to "one's original shape," that is, return to one's authentic nature.

Resilience deepens and becomes more accessible as modulation and regulation of emotional states occur and as cognitive capacities develop. Suffering can build or uncover resilience, but *only if* there is a safe haven of supportive relationships as well as cultural beliefs and traditions that maintain hope and perseverance.

In terms of the healing power of a therapeutic relationship, there is a direct correlation between vulnerability and resilience. Uncovering the resilient core within our patients is both a retrieval process as well as a co-creative discovery process, one that requires the exposure of the patient's vulnerability in order to heal old wounds and feelings of shame. Understanding the interconnections between shame and vulnerability, and vulnerability and resilience are key theoretical touchstones of this book.

As each patient embarks on his or her therapeutic journey, there is no formulaic or theoretical framework that can claim superiority over others. Rather, good therapy is an increasing amalgamation of skills and relational honesty. It is fraught with risk and uncertainty, where painful memories and tender surprises are uncovered as the bond of the imperfect therapeutic relationship strengthens and allows for more of the real self to be revealed.

Initially, the therapist holds the optimism, determination, patience, and confidence that *change is possible*. The belief that change is possible relies on a belief in resilience, notwithstanding negative circumstances, early attachment failures, trauma, or neglect. The resilience of the real self becomes stronger and more sure-footed through the mirroring, patience, safety, and trust in the bond created through the therapeutic relationship. As David Whyte reminds us, *"Let your vulnerabilities be this time not a weakness but a faculty for understanding what's about to happen."*

OUR THEORETICAL APPROACH TO RESILIENCE AND THE THERAPEUTIC CHANGE PROCESS

The recent appearance of the concept of resilience in dynamic treatment is a significant metapsychological advance in our understanding of the complex nature of inner change. The complexity of change is made a little less complex when we recognize growth as a dialectic outcome of the therapeutic encounter between our core *real* selves and our idealized protective selves, that is to say, the encounter between the authentic self and the *false* self.

The metapsychological advance involves the idea that from the very beginning of life, the mind (like the body) is in a continuing process of working to actualize itself. The process is inherent. It is not just a wish to get well but a built-in need *we all share* to get well. The process is seldom easy and often very challenging, especially as defensive structures are more heavily entrenched. But the crucial shift in thinking is in the awareness that the real self is *always* present no matter how submerged, disconnected, or discounted it may be. As Russell (2015) expresses it, "Our deepest fear is not that we are inadequate. Our deepest fear is that we are powerful beyond measure. It is our light, not our darkness that most frightens us" (p. 3).

This metapsychological appreciation compels us more and more to be attuned to the patient's therapeutic moment, as patients desperately deal with unintegrated splits, which have historically robbed them of their vitality, resourcefulness, and sense of being. As we learn to stay with the patient in the immediate moment, we subjectively experience the vulnerability of despair and hopelessness. This is the intersubjective posture linked to the therapeutic alliance to which we will continually refer.

Lest this sound like a formula for therapeutic overload, it is this very *change in posture* that liberates us to monitor and process moment-to-moment information as the patient shifts from self-state to self-state. Since we are working every moment monitoring disconnected or dissociated states, we stay more alive in our ability to sustain ourselves in both the short and long run. Both patient and therapist benefit from this aliveness, which is our best therapeutic ally to productive work and our best insurance against "burnout."

Just how can we protect ourselves from burnout and compassion fatigue? The protection comes from how we see change. Throughout this Workbook, therapeutic change is seen as the result of a resurrection of the patient's authentic (real) self. This is true no matter what level of pathology we encounter. Our moment-to-moment resonance with even the most bedeviled real self keeps us in touch with what is possible. Optimism for our patients and for the work we do is the result.

It is inevitable that we have joined the emerging focus among practitioners of patient resilience. This is not a Pollyanna-ish blindness to tragedy, nor is it a blindness to increasing levels of narcissistic pathology in our society. Rather it is a description of an approach to treatment (and especially treatment of character pathology) that is both more promising and more sustaining than previous attempts, either short-term or long-term.

However, we must be careful not to see resilience as a brand new approach we are just discovering. In her otherwise highly instructive book, Russell (2015) writes that because of denial in the field, we have "not had a word" for resilience capacity or resilient potential. This assumption of newness is not warranted. It may feel like a new approach to treatment from the view of classical thinking. However, the work of Karen Horney, in particular, identified just this very approach to treating character pathology and associated disorders of the self. Horney's psychoanalytic institute has been recommending and refining just this experience-near empathic understanding of treatment for well over the last half century. She explicitly focused on the alienation from the real self as the origin of most psychic distress and described real self as the " 'original' force toward individual growth and fulfillment" (Horney, 1950, p. 158).

Resilience has not been well-accepted in therapeutic circles until recently. It is not a novel idea, but it has been marginalized because of political struggles and entrenched biases in the field. The current work of Fosha, Russell, and others may help to overcome these historic internecine conflicts.

AN INTRODUCTION TO THE STRUCTURE OF THIS WORKBOOK

This text is designed as a follow-up Workbook directly amplifying teaching and training concepts from our text *Listening with Purpose: Entry Points into Shame and Narcissistic Vulnerability* (2012). The Workbook provides detailed case examples to clarify theoretical concepts and techniques. Our aim is to enable therapists to sort through difficult clinical issues, finding anew further efficacy of treatment. We provide an extensive sampling of videotaped case vignettes and study/discussion questions throughout each chapter. As a stand-alone document, this Workbook does not replace supervision but is meant to capture as closely as possible the unfolding experiential reality and challenges of the treatment process as conveyed through the medium of the printed page. We believe our constructivist approach is readily adaptable to a variety of treatment approaches and will be of benefit to trainees and early career clinicians, as well as seasoned practitioners.

GOALS OF THE WORKBOOK

Our goals in developing this Workbook are to provide clinicians with tools to:

- Improve clinical assessment and intervention techniques.
- Enhance therapeutic listening skills.
- Develop greater confidence around the "timing" of interventions.
- Maximize growth opportunities through deepening the therapeutic relationship.
- Leverage both positive and negative transference to repair insecure or traumatic attachments.

- Identify micro-dissociations as blocking mechanisms that dampen down awareness in moments of stress.
- Assist patients in the consolidation of gains and the identification of resilience throughout the treatment process.

The bulleted items capture aspects of what it means to attend to the entire scope of clinical practice. Each element constitutes a critical aspect of treatment, a "part" of a larger whole. As such, our constructivist approach to psychotherapy requires a systemic-relational framework, one that draws the therapists' attention to various components of listening and moment-to-moment tracking as the treatment unfolds.

The Workbook draws from here-and-now experiential illustrations of theoretical concepts and process techniques that come from a modern, broad-based psychodynamic-relational orientation. However, cognitive-behavioral therapists and other practitioners who have used our approach to treatment have reported that the process grid and the foundational techniques underlying it have immediate applicability to their work as well. Treatment goals and intervention techniques can be easily modified to the therapist's background and training. The process-oriented model presented in this manual offers a comprehensive picture of the psyche and easily integrates relational, intrapsychic, and systemic (or contextual) information into the frame. If the therapist is able to hold the interconnected systemic framework, then any particular intervention has an enhanced chance of having lasting effects, which will certainly include progress in uncovering the resilient core.

The Four Quadrant Model we have created presents the therapist with a psychic roadmap that highlights recurrent shame as a driving force behind most defensively based behaviors and beliefs. With this model and our experience-near approach, we illustrate how shame and attempts to compensate for feelings of shame become a unifying factor in helping to explain most dissociative and narcissistically driven defenses.

Patients enter treatment because they experience painful injuries or wounds to their basic sense of self. These range from patients who suffer from episodic struggles around self-worth, to patients with a significant history of trauma, abuse, deprivation, or insecure attachment. Clinicians who work with a wide variety of symptom presentations will find this model relevant and most useful.

We hope you use this book as a personal reference or a jumping off point for discussion in small group peer supervision or within the context of formal supervision. We also trust that the Workbook will be a resource that you can refer to as needed to help refine your skills as a therapist or to help sort through difficult sessions or "stuck moments" in treatment.

By way of beginning, here is a sample video that will give you a taste of what we are talking about. Excerpts from this video will also be reintroduced in Chapter 4 after key concepts have been explained.

Please refer to the Routledge website at www.routledge.com/book/97811381 83285, Video 1.1: Consultation Session on Learning to Trust the Process.

Questions for Discussion

1. In this video, the supervisee talks about slowing the therapeutic listening process by tracking words that become entry points. We will clarify the concept of entry points in Chapter 5. As a beginning, what do you think she means by learning to trust the process?

2. How might staying grounded in the present develop increased curiosity and powers of observation?

3. What do you think that the supervisee means by "the music that accompanies the words"?

This video provides a partial orientation and introduction to the concepts and process methodologies that will be highlighted throughout this Workbook. Certainly, a key point is to direct the reader to the interconnected relationship between resilience and the compensatory protective measures used to hide feelings of shame and vulnerability. Resilience grows as the therapeutic process gradually brings these compensatory measures into conscious awareness. Furthermore, with increased self-awareness, the patient is able to understand how former defensive attempts can be modified in the service of facilitating the patient's emerging health and authenticity.

ORGANIZATION OF THE WORKBOOK

This treatment manual will present an explicit application of our Four Quadrant Model, originally introduced in our first book, *Listening with Purpose: Entry Points into Shame and Narcissistic Vulnerability* (2012). Our Workbook enables clinicians to increase their understanding and gain confidence in how to use the model to formulate more effective and timely intervention strategies. The Workbook is organized as follows:

- We will begin with a review of underlying principles and working assumptions that inform our experience-near approach to treatment.
- This will be followed by a review of the importance of Character Formation and Character Solutions (or pseudo-solutions) to compensate for feelings of alienation.
- We will then provide a detailed review of the Four Quadrant Model, covering and integrating each quadrant. The goal is to have a working understanding and application of how to use the model as an assessment instrument and how to best intervene in the unfolding treatment.
- Specific focus on moment-to-moment tracking, part-whole analysis, transference, and the range of dissociative phenomena will be covered in subsequent chapters.
- Each chapter will provide brief written case vignettes as well as accompanying video illustrations that can be accessed through a secure password on the Routledge website. These case examples highlight concepts and process techniques to improve and deepen the quality of therapeutic listening.
- There will be questions, analyses, and worksheets along with accompanying video case illustrations to help integrate major concepts covered in our text.
- All of the videos used in this Workbook are a consolidation of actual case material that has been edited or compressed for teaching purposes.

LET'S BEGIN WITH A FEW WORKING ASSUMPTIONS

The approach used in this Workbook is based on several critically important and unifying assumptions. Treatment interventions are based on *tracking the therapeutic dialogue in the present moment*. Historical material becomes relevant, as it is connected to ongoing struggles and repeating patterns that continue to manifest in the present, both relationally and intrapsychically.

The underpinnings of our approach are as follows:

- The term "narcissistic injury" is defined *not* as a set of DSM or ICD-10 diagnostic symptoms. Rather, it is seen as a formidable residue of characterological damage that is active (or activated) in the present moment.
- The concept of narcissistic injury is understood on a continuum, where degrees of injury correlate to levels of fragility and vulnerability, all of which interfere with spontaneity, resilience, and authentic self-emergence.

- The treatment of narcissistic injury involves the here-and-now unpacking of the complex construction of narcissistic defenses, in particular its characterological residue.
- Narcissistic injury is not created in a vacuum but is based on early (or later) failures of attachment. Narcissistic compensations are attempts to maintain precarious attachments, as well as to bolster a fragile sense of self.
- Our aim throughout the treatment process is to neutralize painful feelings of shame by creating a therapeutic healing environment based on a secure attachment to the therapist.
- Over-determined and compulsively driven "solutions" (or organizing schemas) are forms of dissociative or vertical splitting. Therefore, these defenses interfere with the emergence of authenticity and adult growth throughout the life span.
- Ongoing treatment involves uncovering dissociations, ranging from micro-dissociative ruptures to more severe episodes of dissociative splitting that are the by-products of insecure attachment and traumatic injury.
- Our treatment approach is "experience-near," one that requires interactive, focused attention in the present moment. This moment-to-moment immersion into our patients' subjective experience is what enables us to sense and uncover dissociated states that operate in the present moment.
- Engaging in the present moment is also what enables us to deepen our sense of connectedness with our patients with the aim of creating experiences of secure attachment, which in turn strengthens a sense of resilience and emerging authenticity.
- Since dissociation is a self-protective "habit" or an "energy-conserving" neurological response in reaction to early empathic failures, the intervention strategies offered in this Workbook are frequently aimed at right-brain-to-right-brain communication.

In order for psychotherapy to be a vehicle for meaningful, healing contact around narcissistic injury, treatment requires a non-linear approach, one that attends to the "right brain" language of emotion, vocal tone, the pace of our response, and what it means to "be with" the patient. As such, these ten underpinnings of our treatment approach draw upon recent advances in attachment theory as it applies to systemic/relational psychotherapy. The correlation between styles of learned attachment and neurophysiological advances connecting brain development and affect-regulation represents the integration of multiple disciplines. Attachment theory allows for a wider range of psychological disturbances to come into view in a way that is also anchored in relational psychodynamic therapy. Such theory becomes a unifying lens wherein problems presented in therapy can be clinically tied to problems of living.

RIGHT-BRAIN-TO-RIGHT-BRAIN RESONANCE

The field of neuroscience has drawn us to reexamine *explicit* and *implicit* aspects of the self. Neuroscientific researchers have concluded that the right hemisphere of the brain is linked to *implicit* information processing, whereas the left hemisphere is connected to *explicit* (or more conscious) processing of information. Heilman, Nadeau, and Beversdorf (2003) state, "Because the right and left hemispheres store different forms of knowledge and mediate different forms of cognitive activity, different neuronal architectures probably exist within the association cortices of the hemispheres" (p. 374).

These are welcome contributions from neuroscience because they validate the profound changes that have been occurring in our practice of psychotherapy and psychoanalysis over the past thirty years. The paradigm shift has been instrumental in changing our perspectives from ego to self, object to subject, archeological distance to experience-near, guilt to shame, repression to dissociation, and from discrete psychiatric symptoms to character structure. The paradigm shift outlined has also been fundamental to our understanding of clinical change and to the process of therapeutic listening itself.

Findings in neuroscience are rapidly helping practitioners to overcome their reluctance to see the remarkable contributions that philosophy and metatheory have been making to our everyday practice. The paradigm shift outlined above has been greatly facilitated by our understanding of phenomenology and its power of moment-to-moment tracking of psychic reverberations.

Among those practitioners, in our view, who are most aligned with this paradigm shift are Andrade, Ginot, Levine, McLaughlin, and Schore. Schore (2011), who has made significant contributions integrating neuroscientific findings into clinical application, draws our attention to the importance of *implicit affect*, *implicit communication*, and *implicit self-regulation*. His examination of the critical role that *implicit affect-regulation* has on the organization of the self as well as the therapeutic relationship offers a valuable frame of reference, particularly with regard to our assumptions around the transferential relationship.

Ginot (2007, 2009) is in alignment with Schore and concurs that therapist sensitivity or what has been called right brain attunement to the patient's non-verbal cues is a necessary therapeutic skill to develop. Tuning into implicit processing allows the analyst to connect with that which is yet to be verbalized, while also acting as an implicit regulator of the patient's affective states, both conscious and unconscious. She further states that unconscious self-states and relational patterns triggered by implicit memories and attachment styles have a direct impact on transference-counter-transference dynamics.

Finally, recent contributions from psychodynamically oriented clinicians have commented on the collaboration between neuroscience and the practice of psychotherapy and psychoanalysis. Wachtel (2014) states that "the pursuit of meaning, the hermeneutic quest, is not antithetical to the process of inquiry pursued from an 'external' vantage point" (p. 150). Stressing resilience, Russell (2015) reviews the literature on this dialogue and reminds us that "the brain is non-linear" (p. 189), and this is true whether we are focusing on neuroscience or on psychotherapeutic change.

INTENSIFYING THERAPEUTIC LISTENING

As treatment paradigms shift to "experience-near" and relational models, how we think about therapeutic listening is also changing. Rather than focusing on linear models, where the past informs the present, our belief is that anything that is unresolved historically will reveal itself in the present moment, all within the unfolding dynamic of the therapeutic relationship.

Over the years, it has been interesting to observe how the practice of psychotherapy and meditative practices seem to be converging. Inevitably, that convergence takes place in the present moment. The art of becoming mindful in the present moment requires the development of a skill set that has to do with clearing the obstacles of the mind to become more skillful observers of our surrounding environment and, of course, of our own internal environment. The latter includes predisposed assumptions and training biases, cultural judgments, and personal blind spots.

The moment-to-moment resonance of listening in the present moment can be seen as a discipline not unlike the learned discipline of quieting the mind through mindfulness meditation. As practitioners, when we adopt a stance of working through interferences and less than conscious mechanisms (including rigidly held theoretical assumptions), we open ourselves to a *slower pace* as part of our therapeutic stance.

Slowing the process down is both an *attitude* and a *technique*. It is a basic form of grounding, one that both steadies us and helps to build trust and clinical confidence that the unfolding relational dynamic will provide us with the necessary cues we need. As the process begins to slow down, one of the outcomes of controlling the pace is that patients begin to learn a new rhythm of exchange, one that invites more curiosity, self-reflection, and introspection. In time, this increases confidence, insight, and affect-regulation.

Many clinicians have turned to mindfulness meditation techniques to assist patients with affect-regulation. Various trauma specialists believe that traumatized patients typically cannot tolerate the practice of meditation, as they experience it as initially over-stimulating, even terrifying, flooding the patient with a feeling of fragmentation and emptiness. Although this caution is well-founded, particularly with patients who have more severe trauma histories, the therapeutic relationship can build trust and the necessary skill sets to help with affect-regulation and identity cohesion. Once this occurs, patients seem better able to handle mindfulness meditation practices as well as better able to tolerate the experience of depth psychotherapy. Research is beginning to show that the long-term practice of mindfulness techniques as well as successful psychotherapy can change one's neuro-circuitry as well.

Questions for Review

1. *How might moment-to-moment mindfulness increase the capacity for therapeutic listening?*

2. *We have defined the term "narcissistic injury" as a "formidable residue of characterological damage" that is active (or activated) in the present moment. How do you understand the relationship between narcissistic symptoms and characterologically driven attempts on the part of patients to create internal balance?*

3. *How might this knowledge have an impact on how you view some of your more difficult or fragile patients?*

4. *How do you see the connection between:*

   a. Shame and vulnerability.

   b. Vulnerability and resilience.

5. *If you experience pressure from patients who ask you "to do something to fix their problem," how might slowing the process down help you formulate your response?*

   a. List three responses that you might give if asked the above question.

---

b. What feelings or concerns about performance might be triggered by being asked this question?

c. What else might be occurring dynamically in the treatment at that moment?

SLOWING THE PROCESS DOWN

As therapists, when we slow down the pace of the dialogic interaction, we actually create an *atmospheric change* in the present moment. It is a therapeutic technique that is both subtle and powerful. Let us unpack the essential elements of this process technique:

- Slowing down the process is a way of interrupting automatic, habituated thoughts on the part of the patient *as well as* ourselves.
- Slowing down the process is a way of *being with* the patient that allows us to connect with the patient *right-brain-to-right-brain*. In doing so, we are better able to attend to vocal tone; nuance; and intensity of affect, body language, empathic resonance, and one's overall intersubjective experience.
- Slowing the dialogic process down is a method of monitoring micro-dissociative ruptures that occur within the patient. These can easily be missed by a casual observer either because of their subtle nature or because they are "split-second occurrences."
- Slowing down the pace of the dynamic exchange is a way of modeling affect-regulation for patients who experience rapid or painful spikes in affect.
- Slowing down the process is a technique that can gradually bring to the surface shameful material that is buried, disavowed, or sheltered from view.
- Slowing down the process can help both patient and therapist better identify emerging threads of resilience.
- Slowing down the process allows the therapist to see early signs of therapeutic progress, which enables the therapist to provide a mirroring function in the service of solidifying or consolidating therapeutic gains.
- Properly mirrored, these threads of resilience and therapeutic gains build on themselves to develop increased confidence in one's authentic gifts, talents, and aspirations.

THE CONTEXT OF PACE

By asking questions that encourage patients to fill in the details of their life story in greater depth, we demonstrate a quality of attention that is also a form of permission-giving, one that is both gentle and respectful. This type of experience of "being with" allows the therapist to demonstrate, through careful attention to detail and nuance, how the self develops in relationship.

Introducing a change of pace, a slowing down of the retelling of a patient's narrative, can act as a preparation for what is to come when a patient develops a readiness and trust in being able to recall and recount painful memories. Thus, over time, our questions and careful listening help our patients bring a new curiosity to their own thought processes, beliefs, and assumptions. This type of relational exchange is precisely *how* patients gradually develop more self-reflective capacities. As clinicians have said, "Self-reflection reflects affect-regulation."

The process of self-reflection is certainly complex in origin but it can be developed through healthy relational exchanges. Trauma interrupts a healthy developmental and relational learning curve. With DeYoung (2015), we believe that, "It's not just that our shamed patients lack the linking skills to tell a coherent story; it's also that something tells them it would be dangerous to know it" (p. 113). Yet, on the other hand, the process of psychotherapy creates many leverage points for experience-near, dynamic, deepening self-reflection through mirroring and attentive listening.

When the therapist brings careful attention to the moment-to-moment interaction in the unfolding present, she is *reflecting with* the patient something that then becomes a shared enterprise. With multiple repetitions, the relational dynamic eventually becomes transformed into something that the patient is able to internalize, a relational process exchange that can be encoded in memory, to be used again and again as a self-reflective capacity. As Martha Stark (1999) so aptly states,

Let us begin by thinking about how the therapist positions herself moment by moment in relation to the patient. My intent is to provide the therapist with a way to conceptualize the options available to her as she sits with her patient—with respect both to how she arrives at understanding and to what she says or does.

(p. 3)

Video Case Vignettes: "Slowing the Process Down"

In this next section, two videotape selections are provided to underscore the importance of slowing down the pace of the dialogue. The first video is a brief therapeutic exchange where a patient reveals information that she fears will cast her in a negative light in the therapist's eyes. Notice how the patient speeds up the pace of her conversation in an attempt to distance herself from negative material. The second video offers a brief psycho-educational snapshot that encourages the patient to slow down her own thinking by paying attention to self-descriptive language. The therapist slows the process down by questioning the patient's self-descriptive phrase in order that the patient may ascribe positive aspects to her own resilience. In addition, the therapist's question offers an opportunity for the patient to increase her own awareness around the connection between past and present, especially around her desire to form a secure attachment.

In the first video case vignette, observe how the therapist repeats the word "sneaky," not as a question, but as a reflective statement back to the patient. Repeating a charged word, such as "sneaky," in a neutral voice is both permission-giving and a way of beginning to slow the process down.

Please refer to the Routledge website, Video 1.2: Using Key Words to Slow the Process Down.

Patient: You know, my mother had a devious side to her.

Therapist: Yes?

Patient: It made it difficult to trust anybody. Well, I mean I trust you, of course. But my mother was devious. Actually, she was sneaky.

Therapist: Sneaky.

Patient: I hated her, but I had to hate her in secret. It was MY secret. I always envied people who loved their mother. Life would have been easier for me if I had a loving mother. Do you think it's bad for a person to hate their mother? Oh my God! What must you think of me? Do you think I'm a horrible person for what I just said? Don't answer that. I don't have a right to ask you that. What must you think of me? There I go again rambling. You know my boyfriend says I ramble a lot. Last night he told me that it was hard to keep up with me. I'm not sure what he meant. Do you think that he was secretly trying to let me know that he has a hard time keeping up with me sexually? I do seem to want more physical reassurance than he does. I don't see what's wrong with someone wanting reassurance from her boyfriend. What do you think?

Therapist: What do I think . . . ?

Commentary

In this case scenario, the patient is flooding the session with a variety of comments that deserve much further inquiry. Often, therapists are uncertain where to jump in or which comment to respond to first. If a patient continues with a longer narrative, jumping from topic to topic, many therapists comment on the last statement or question presented by the patient. For example, in this scenario the patient asks the therapist what she thinks about wanting physical reassurance from her boyfriend.

If the therapist responds to the direct question about the boyfriend with a concrete answer, it runs the risk of allowing other dynamic clues to remain unattended by the therapist. For example, earlier in the session, when the therapist slowed the process down by repeating the word "sneaky," the comment opened a portal to the patient's anger. This in turn created a feeling of embarrassment and the need to seek reassurance from the therapist. However, rather than being able to ask directly, the patient speeds up the process, deflecting away from transferential material that needs to be eventually addressed.

There are multiple "entry points" for comment in this patient's brief exchange. However, before making an intervention about *what the patient said*, the therapist would be well served to pause and reflect with the patient upon *the manner and process by which the patient's information is being conveyed*.

Case Example Discussion Questions

1. *List three ways that you could comment on the manner in which the patient is delivering the information in this session. For example:*

   a. *What would be a general statement that you could make to slow the process down?*

   b. *How might you draw out the patient's affect as a way of slowing the process down?*

   c. *How could you inquire in a gentle way about the patient's need for reassurance?*

2. *What might you begin to listen for in terms of secrets, trust, and hidden motives regarding:*

   a. *Transference?*

   b. *What is being kept hidden from the therapy?*

---

c. *Expectations in relationship with others?*

d. *How the patient handles disappointments?*

3. *Discuss how slowing the process down is a critical element in deepening therapeutic listening skills.*

In the following case vignette, the patient and therapist are talking about resilience as it pertains to one's history, basic temperament, and capacity for developing a secure attachment. You will note that the therapist weaves into the discussion the importance of the mirroring function of attachment as an aspect of the healing power of the therapy experience. From a psychodynamic perspective, the therapist *systemically holds* the dynamic tension both between and within the patient's psychic states. These states include defensive coping mechanisms, the patient's attachment and character style, and the increasing emergence of authenticity and resilience.

Please refer to the Routledge website, Video 1.3: Resilience in the Process of Psychotherapy.

Patient: Last week we were talking about resilience. I was thinking about that a lot, particularly when you commented that I was very resilient. When I thought about it after our session, it made me cry.

Therapist: It made you cry?

Patient: I mean it was a good cry. (Pause) I had always thought about myself as a survivor. But somehow seeing myself as resilient shifts something in me. It shifts how I appreciate myself. Resilient feels more positive; it describes my strength of character, as opposed to just surviving an awful childhood.

Therapist: It sounds like you're saying that resilience describes something that's inside you, not just something that occurred because of luck or happenstance.

Patient: Yes, exactly. That's exactly it. So, I wanted to ask you, what makes someone resilient? Is it all about temperament? Is it something you're just born with?

16

Therapist: I wouldn't necessarily say that resilience and temperament are the same thing, but I do think that resilience as a *capacity* is something that everyone is born with.

Patient: Well, I've been thinking about my childhood and the difference between my brother and me. He made a successful life for himself financially, but he never got over his resentment. He resents how we grew up, and he resents me. He's an angry and depressed person, and I think he resents me for moving beyond our family. He allowed his childhood to own him. I don't want that to be me. I can't stand my ex-husband, but I don't want that negative experience to own me. I want to get beyond that.

Therapist: Did your brother ever go into therapy?

Patient: Oh, no. He feels that therapy is a bunch of junk.

Therapist: So, one of the differences between the two of you is that you reached out for help. I think that's a key element in resilient people. If we've been hurt or deprived or traumatized, it takes some internal resilience or basic trust to reach out to others. This is especially true for you because your parental figures were so disappointing and chaotic. Yet, somehow, you were able to go outside of your nuclear family to engage in a different kind of relational experience through your therapy. You see, resilience can be a basic capacity we are all born with, but when bad things happen, it takes a benign "other" to support who you are, to see your innate strengths and capacities so that you can recover from the hurt or damage. The therapy relationship is a form of mirroring or permission-giving that is a confirmation that who you are is important, that you are seen and have a right to grow and live into your capacities.

Patient: You know, when I was a young girl, I had this vivid memory of walking down the street in NYC holding the hand of an adult; I think it was my father. I don't know why, but I decided to smile at strangers, not as a manipulative ploy, but it was a form of trying to find alternative connections. It worked. People smiled back. They seemed kind, and it didn't take much to get their attention.

Therapist: Yes, that's a wonderful example of early resilience and curiosity about the world.

Patient: I have this image that there was another child holding my father's other hand, my brother holding his other hand. But he was just passively walking along. My brother just decided to take what he was given. Maybe I was always just a little more rebellious.

Therapist: Rebellious?

Patient: I didn't mean rebellious in a negative way, more like a refusal to give in to being made to feel invisible.

Therapist: So are you saying that part of your resilience was contained in your spirit of rebelliousness?

Patient: Yes, I guess so.

Therapist: I'm wondering if we could find a different word, other than rebelliousness.

Patient: Yes, yes. I like that idea. (Long pause, thinking) How about tenacity, or fighting spirit, (another pause), or (quieter voice) or maybe my own inner knowing, knowing when something wasn't right somehow?

Questions for Discussion

1. *Discuss your thoughts on the value of the therapist using resilience as a "psychoeducational opportunity."*

2. *By shifting from seeing the patient's progress as something that could be attributed to luck or temperament, what doorways of reflection and insight is the patient able to offer?*

3. *How is reaching out for help a key component to building one's capacity for resilience?*

4. *Why do you think the therapist challenged the patient around associating her resilience with rebelliousness?*

In this final video in Chapter 1, we want to share a frequently asked question we receive from beginning therapists. When tracking the therapeutic dialogue, beginning clinicians often are at a loss as to what to say next. The following video with accompanying analysis will speak to this question.

Please refer to the Routledge website, Video 1.4: What Do I Say Next?

Patient: I'm always getting into **QUARRELS**.
Therapist: What happens?
Patient: I always seem to have a **DISAGREEMENT** with people.
Therapist: Is it about everything?
Patient: It's about the same things all the time.
Therapist: It's about the same things? Can you talk about those things?
Patient: Well, it makes me **UPSET** to think about those things.
Therapist: I see. How do you get when you are upset?
Patient: I get **ANGRY** but I don't like to think about feelings like that.
Therapist: What happens when you think about feelings like that?
Patient: I get very **ANXIOUS** about what people are going to think.
Therapist: You mean if you get angry, it makes you anxious to think that people won't like you?
Patient: Something like that. They won't **APPROVE** of me. They won't respect me.
Therapist: So you have a lot of disagreements, but they seem to be dangerous for you.
Patient: Yes, I'd rather not have them at all.
Therapist: I guess it seems to you that if you could get rid of disagreements, then you wouldn't have all these other awful feelings.
Patient: That's right. Can you help me get rid of disagreements?
Therapist: Well, people can't think the same all the time. I disagree with people sometimes.
Patient: Does it upset you?
Therapist: No. I say how I see things; I give my opinion. Some people agree with me, and some people disagree with me. I feel it's my responsibility to make myself as clear as I can, but I'm not responsible for the other person's reaction. Do you know what I mean?
Patient: I wish I were that way.
Therapist: We get that way by doing just what we are doing now—talking about how these things really make us feel.

Analysis

The question "But what do I say next?" is among the most commonly asked questions by therapists early in their training. It is a puzzling question for them because it is actually a "process" question hoping against hope for a "content" answer. Under the surface, the question involves a number of critical process issues that we highlight in this training exercise. How do we convert dialogue content to therapeutic process? Patients are frequently more at ease describing external situations rather than internal experience. Especially difficult are emotionally charged states of minds.

A typical way patients handle stress is to psychologically move fast to override frightening or distressing material. As trainers, we have been teaching trainees the importance of how to "slow the process down" in real time. This can involve asking process-oriented questions geared specifically to the immediate content. Inevitably the patient will start to try to put into words stressful internal moments, a process that can happen quickly or can take considerable time. As this process becomes engaged, the process itself begins to slow down, and what we have called "entry points" become manifest. These are points that the therapist intuitively feels will provide significant entry into the patient's inner dynamics.

Learning how to *listen* for language that may telegraph that something possibly lies under the surface is what we mean by finding an "entry point." The process of learning *what to say next* requires the therapist to develop a skill set where he or she uses the patient's language or turn of phrase as a way to track *process dynamics*. Tracking what the patient says in the present moment allows us to not only attend to affective material that is not explicitly expressed through the actual content of what is being said, it also allows for the therapist to gradually probe for what is being hidden from view. A more detailed elaboration as to how to access hidden material by drawing upon *entry points* will be discussed in Chapter 5.

We introduce this clinical vignette at the beginning of the Workbook because we want to set the stage for how one can attend to a listening process in a way that slows the process down in the present moment. By doing so, we are helping bring into conscious awareness a shift from the patient's habituated responses and reflexive patterns to a way of engaging in dialogue with another that increases *curiosity and self-reflection*. These two attributes or capacities help the therapist join with patients in a way that enables them to share in the responsibility and discovery of what it takes to achieve emotional repair and growth.

As you will see in this training video, we have identified our educated guesses of entry points for this patient and highlighted them in bold. Note the therapist's response after each putative entry point. Gently as possible, the therapist tries to enlist the patient in the "here and now" of the patient's idiosyncratic story rather than the "there and then." Note how the patient moves gradually into more emotional terrain from Quarrels to Disagreement to Upset to Anger to Anxiousness to (dis)Approval. The process is clearly non-linear and non-sequential with therapeutic progress linked to fitting parts to a larger characterological whole. Thus, each entry point, once confirmed, is organically connected to every other entry point, as will be clear in our Workbook.

Questions for Discussion

1. How would you describe the role the therapist is playing?

2. Discuss your understanding of the difference between process tracking and content tracking.

3. In this videotaped case vignette, how does the therapist use the patient's language with a follow-up response that invites the patient to give further clarifying information?

4. What was your reaction to the therapist sharing a personal disclosure for psycho-educational purposes?

5. Think about one of your more difficult cases, one in which the patient may speak rapidly or jump from topic to topic. How might you use the technique of tracking entry point language to help slow the process down?

SUMMARY

From a philosophical vantage point, the art and science of contemporary psychotherapy implies an active, interactive, and mutual investment in the connective moment. This mutual investment is what comprises the glue of connectivity—something that is *often* non-verbally felt and *never* perfect in its unfolding. The process requires intentionality, attention without preconceived bias, and trust in the shared wisdom that can emerge out of the therapeutic process. This inter-subjective theoretical position asks that the therapist relinquish postures of hierarchy or detachment. In exchange, the therapist is afforded new avenues of immersion, thus creating a deeper understanding of the complex layers of the patient's awareness, conflicts, and desires.

Immersion as a process is present-focused; it is very dynamic and mutable. One way of understanding the complex process of immersion is to describe it as empathically *leaning into* the patient's subjective experience. This includes a combination of the patient's developmental history, perceived family dynamics, current interpersonal and intrapsychic tensions, and assessment of psychological resilience. These components are woven into an evolving understanding that is shaped by the subjectivity of the therapist's lens, which includes the therapist's own prior dynamics. As a rule, the posture of immersion has been shown to reduce objectifying trends in the therapist's personality, as it requires a continual checking in for confirmation from the patient during the process of the therapy.

Staying within the present moment, slowing down the process, and confirming or disproving assumptions are foundational postures we encourage you to take. Throughout the remaining chapters of this book, it is our hope that you trust your increasing capacity to be able to *lean into the process*.

2

The Importance of Character

[The realizing self is felt] and we can say that every glimpse we get of it feels more real, more certain, more definite than anything else. We can observe this quality in ourselves or in our patients when . . . there is a release from the grip of some compulsive need.
—Horney (1950, p. 158)

Thus, what has now become a deeply ingrained aspect of my own cognitive style—to construct first, however tentatively, a hypothesis concerning the structure of the patient's nuclear self, an outline of its central program, of the basic means by which the program is to be realized, and only subsequently to assess such details as psychic mechanisms against the background of this tentative overview of the personality—seems to be scientifically justified.
—Kohut (1984, p. 127)

The importance of character seems to have fallen out of favor in the field's recent efforts to adopt a more empathic, relationally attuned stance with patients. For many clinicians, the notion of character is often misunderstood, seen as something fixed or archaic, merely attributed to individuals with Axis II personality disorders. Yet, characterological forces are at play within *every* moment and within *every* treatment exchange.

When we consider character and character structure, several questions immediately come to mind. For example, is character merely the sum of coexisting "self-states," which are more or less at peace with each other? How might we assess the degree to which the various self-states are consciously connected or disconnected from one another? In other words, can an individual's character structure remain integrated when he or she vividly describes a self-standing "helpless self" that appears to be disconnected from an equally familiar "hated self," both of which seem to be "forgotten" when the individual draws upon a strongly held "idealized self"?

Inherent within the importance of character is the idea that acutely conflicting components of the self are continuously fueling and reinforcing each other at all levels of consciousness, thereby integrating themselves into a structure at war within itself. DeRosis (1974) called this a precariously balanced and stress-filled *invented self* and Winnicott (1960), emphasizing the pseudo-resolution involved, described it as a *false self*.

One of the tasks of therapy is to look for where and how these various self-states manifest over time. When we begin to understand how apparently separate self-states can coexist within the personality, we open the doorway of understanding how character shapes motivations, symptoms, relational expectations—in others words, the intersubjective field. Aspects of the intersubjective landscape include attending to the patient's:

- Over-determined efforts to succeed.
- Fears of failure or disappointment.
- Feelings of underlying shame or vulnerability.
- Ways in which the person disconnects from painful affect.
- Expectations of others in a relationship.
- Level of resilience.
- Degree of self-care.

Deeper listening keeps the therapist in touch with these multiple aspects of the self—both the conscious and the hidden, the syntonic and the dystonic. As the therapist "holds" more and more of the whole, the patient internally also begins to hold more and more of the self.

OVERVIEW

Character solutions constitute an alienation from the self—the deeper the alienation, the more severe the character disturbance. Yet, our clinical experience shows us that character organization is manifestly mutable, not fixed. Defensively driven character organization is something that is highly sensitive to context and to the evolution of therapeutic work. Mutability of character within the treatment context is seen through the unfolding transference as well as within the therapeutic alliance. As DeYoung (2015) summarizes, "[C]haracter solutions are performative. The interpersonal and the intrapsychic are an integrated system, performing self-in-relation in the here-and-now. We come to know our clients' past not through archeological retrieval but through the organization of our clients' performance of this self in relation with us" (p. 146).

The term "solutions" has many important implications for psychodynamic psychotherapy. The term is meant to capture a description of the patient's own attempt at solving his or her problems. Therefore, character solutions are frantic attempts at adaptation. Framed as such, our hope is that this will allow for a new paradigm for understanding and treating character pathology. Character solutions are created as a valiant effort by the patient to deal with overwhelming fear and painfully unmet needs. When the problems do not go away, the compulsive creations build on themselves to create a more rigidly "perfect" solution. At some point, the internal conflicts become unmanageable, and the patient becomes flooded with distressing psychological or bodily symptoms. It is often at this moment that the patient comes to us for help.

A further implication can certainly be drawn. Since the character *pseudo-solution* had been developed out of the patient's unmet needs, the process of psychotherapy actually enables the patient to eventually realize that the *solution* came out of desperate need, not out of "badness" or "inferiority." The insight becomes increasingly contextualized: mother's incapacity to nurture in critical ways, father's rigid coldness, or a younger sibling's physical illness ("Is it right to meet my needs if no one else's needs are being met?").

Character is clearly evident in both micro-exchanges and in larger repeating patterns of behaviors and beliefs. Character organization, in effect, describes how the parts of psychic organization fit together to comprise an intrapsychic and relational whole.

When we render character pathology as now a self-made character solution, we place both the patient and ourselves in a more optimistic frame. A sense of authentic self develops and challenges the pseudo-self, first gingerly and then more confidently. Clinical backlashes become more understandable, not as a return to "badness" but as growing pains. Instead of pessimism building on itself, now optimism builds on itself. We might say that the paradigm shift we are describing involves the growing pains of our deeper understanding of our work in both psychodynamic psychotherapy and psychoanalysis (See Horney, 1950).

Character organization, or what has come to be called organizing schemas (Stolorow, Brandchaft, & Atwood, 1987), has become part of how we understand and recognize transference from a relational perspective. All organizing schemas are shaped by systemic-relational exchanges from past to present and are part of an evolving process, transference being no exception.

If we fail to attend to characterological aspects of the personality organization, treatment often stays superficial at best; the therapist can become blindsided by unforeseen complications in the therapy, sometimes causing negative transferential ruptures in the treatment. (We wish to underscore that tying transference to character constitutes a significant break from its drive-derived origins.)

THERAPEUTIC COSTS OF UNDER-ATTENTION TO CHARACTER STRUCTURE

Specific risks associated with under-attention to character structure are as follows:

- Under-attention runs the risk of focusing on a *part* of the person, not the complexity of the *systemic whole*.

- Therapeutic strategies may exclusively focus on the treatment of symptoms without attending to characterological defenses, thereby creating a revolving door, crisis-driven approach to treatment.
- Symptoms are often a protective breach in an individual's attempts to maintain a defensively driven homeostatic balance. Focusing exclusively on symptom relief results in a lost opportunity to integrate cut-off parts of the psyche into the whole personality.
- The dynamic of transferential enactments can best be understood through grounding ourselves in an understanding of character. Transferential reactions are one window into the therapist's ability to monitor various self-states within the patient.
- Giving credence to character dynamics is vital because it gives us a systemic and relational appreciation of how self-states are in conflict moment-to-moment. These become visible through the dynamic exchange between patient and therapist.
- In addition, social, cultural, and ethnic factors create unequal power balances between therapist and patient and can contribute to powerful transferential upsurges. These are potentially registered in the subjective moment as well.

Character structure both fuels and is fueled by non-conscious organizing schemas. Indeed structure and schema constitute a systemic whole. Under-attention to any of the above factors comprising a patient's character structure can create a missed opportunity to bring split-off elements of shameful and hidden feelings to the surface. Grasping the intrinsic connections between character, transference, and symptom presentation can be of great clinical value in the ongoing assessment and treatment phases of therapy. They allow the identification of split-off parts and their integration into a cohesive whole, thereby therapeutically addressing the attendant pain that underlies one's (narcissistic) vulnerabilities.

REFINING OUR UNDERSTANDING OF CHARACTER: CHARACTER SOLUTION AS OPPOSED TO CHARACTER DISORDER

Contrary to the DSM view where character is understood as something that is *fixed*, relational models use an intersubjective or process-oriented view and therefore see character as something that is *mutable*. The mutability of character formation is grounded in the belief that change occurs through the unfolding of the patient/therapist relationship. This means that the therapeutic relationship, by its very nature, has the power to impact and shape character throughout the treatment. Hence, character is something that is subject to *context* and the *therapeutic holding environment*.

Karen Horney (1950) coined the term "character solution" to capture both the defensive adaptations that individuals put into place in an attempt to compensate for feelings of shame and vulnerability, as well as the mutability of character organization as it is impacted by the therapeutic encounter. Grounding herself in the perspective of "selfhood," Horney (1945, 1950) believed that failures in relational attachment in childhood mark the beginning of narcissistic disturbances.

- The definition of character solution involves a compulsively driven set of dynamic beliefs and behaviors. Although elements may be part of the person's temperament or hard wiring, the solution itself is a compulsively driven and constantly reinforced way of dealing with others or with oneself.
- Solutions are created in an attempt to overcompensate for internal feelings of inadequacy or lack of safety, or to protect against the eruption of painful psychological conflict. They are conscious, non-conscious, or unconscious attempts to keep uncomfortable feelings at bay.
- Contrary to the Axis I/Axis II approach to organization, where there is a definitional separation between symptom-focused presentations and character disturbances, our view is that virtually all symptom complaints involve some dimension of character; that is, they have some compulsively driven component.

Although less focused on organizing schemas and character structure, attachment theorists are also clearly espousing the basic understanding that systemic-relational exchanges are fundamental to change. From the perspective of attachment theory, qualities of effective caregiving will generally predict conditions that will lead to the authentic development of self. Measures of *affective competence* (Fosha, 2000) include the ability to soothe, mirror, offer appropriate containment, and reflect on emotional experience, the caregiver's own and that of the child's. In addition, Fosha states that effective caregiving is anchored in "actively helping the child with stressful and distressing situations, which are beyond their resources to manage" (Fosha, 2003, p. 227).

Conversely, if a caregiver's affective competence is compromised, there is an inability on the caregiver's part to attune to the child in a way that helps the child learn dyadic affect-regulation. The result of this attachment misalignment "makes it necessary for the child to institute *defense mechanisms to compensate for such caregiving lapses*, leading to insecure attachment organization, or disorganized attachment states of mind, when even defensive efforts fail" (Fosha, 2003, p. 227).

Attachment theory, therefore, includes an appreciation of how defensive postures created in childhood are valiant attempts to compensate for failures within the attachment bond. They are adaptive attempts to reestablish safety and emotional equilibrium when the dyadic relationship fails to provide proper attunement. In our view, if properly approached systemically, relational homeostasis itself can never be "split off" from intrapsychic homeostasis. Interpersonal *and* intrapsychic homeostasis form one system. This is an important training issue, and we will affirm its importance through many clinical examples unfolding in our text.

Defensive compensations possess a compulsive quality. Over time, these compulsive compensations often become more fixed. Unless therapeutic interventions help ameliorate these self-defeating patterns, the individual must rely on old defense mechanisms for stability. Neborsky (2003) highlights the function that compulsive behaviors serve, stating, "Compulsion is predictable, stable, and reliable—albeit rigid, and maladaptive. . . . Therefore, the compulsive behavior compensates for the missing capacity to support and soothe oneself in the face of adversity" (pp. 296–297).

In our introduction we described the emerging convergence between attachment theorists and systemic researchers. The convergence allows us to relationally track the formation of what Horney described as "a character solution" over sixty years ago. Like Horney, who saw these solutions as mutable, not fixed, attachment theorists similarly see the therapeutic relationship as providing a "curative" factor for insecure or disorganized attachments. That is, over time, the consistently safe holding environment created within the treatment context can provide relational opportunities for the patient to experience emotional *attunement*, as well as the inevitable *disruption of attunement*.

Therapeutic missteps or transferential disappointments contribute to inevitable micro-disruptions of attunement. However, when the therapist is able to demonstrate adequate affective competence, the ability to *repair* the connection can occur. Thus, over time, these episodes of connection, disconnection, and successful repair deepen a patient's capacity for a more secure attachment and more authentic sense of self.

DISTINGUISHING BETWEEN CHARACTER SOLUTIONS AND THE REAL SELF

When the clinician initially formulates a dynamic assessment of the patient, a systemic process of differentiating between defensively constructed character postures and the nascent authentic self is critical. Assessing where there are pockets of resilience uncontaminated by despair or hopeless resignation is a major factor in allowing us to identify and hold the dialectic tension between "warring factions" within the person. The ongoing ability to differentiate between health and non-health not only helps inform treatment goals, it factors into how firmly or tenuously the therapeutic relationship will be established. As we will see in future chapters, this awareness itself creates optimism in the therapist and reduces our compassion fatigue.

Throughout training, we encourage the therapist to look for "disconnected splits" between the authentic self and the overcompensated *false* self. The differentiation becomes a solid leverage point for introducing intellectual curiosity and self-reflection to the therapy process.

The therapist is able to develop a greater awareness of disconnected splits that appear within the patient's presentation by marking where contradictions occur within the dialogue.

Here are several examples of disconnected splits:

- A person may say he is the smartest or most productive member of a team, but he becomes angry and slighted when every accomplishment isn't noticed or praised.
- An individual may tell the therapist that she doesn't like being in the "limelight" but reports in great detail all her efforts that go unnoticed and unappreciated.
- A person describes herself as kind-hearted and hating conflict but often resorts to subtle forms of devaluing and dismissing others' accomplishments.
- An individual gets caught lying to his spouse about an affair and justifies his behavior by saying that it wasn't really an affair because he wasn't in love with that person.

Video Case Vignettes

In the next two video case illustrations, you will see examples of varying degrees of disconnected splits within the character organization.

In the first case vignette, the patient is extremely defended in a number of areas: a. the fragile treatment alliance, b. his attempts to hide feelings of vulnerability, c. breakthrough symptoms, which create attempts at reestablishing the grandiose position versus feelings of rage and the devaluation of people who try to usurp his power.

In the second case vignette, we see a patient who has been in treatment for two years. We see positive evidence where her ability to bring her own self-reflective capacities to confront her high standards around achievement are in the service of integrating the disconnected splits within the personality.

These two examples are offered to highlight the range of disconnection and resultant over-determined efforts used to maintain a homeostatic balance in self-image.

Please refer to the Routledge website, Video 2.1: "Rupert"—When Expansive Overcompensation Fails.

The first video depicts a retired business executive coming into treatment for intense repeating nightmares of his corporation being taken over by his former underlings. Although he has been on anti-depression medication for a year, this video describes a brief segment of his psychotherapy early in treatment.

The patient exhibits signs of a markedly expansive character structure given to self-inflation and investment in mastery. As you watch this video, what issues does treating this type of patient bring into focus? How would one think about creating a therapeutic alliance?

Clinical Discussion

1. How can we explain the acutely dystonic nature of this patient's dreams?

2. What are the issues involved in dealing with such split-off emotions?

3. Amidst such extreme polarization of emotions, how can the patient be supported?

4. How can the therapist become more deeply immersed in conflicting self-states without losing personal boundaries?

5. How can such immersion contribute to identifying resilience and emerging signs of the authentic self?

Analysis

The therapist appears to be having some success in connecting the self-states by siding with the patient on the patient's expressed goal of "fighting back." The therapist puts into words the unacceptability of "no words coming out" when the patient wants to fight. By giving language to the patient's frustration and

THE IMPORTANCE OF CHARACTER

confusion, the therapist is able to join the patient around his conflict without any loss of personal boundaries.

Notice that the therapist moves from the intrapsychic to the relational present with the question, "What do your wife and children think about this?" The therapist has moved from the inside to the outside, from the internal to the external. Whenever this type of shift occurs, the question of the timing is worthy of further reflection. For example, one might wonder whether the timing of this question is a distraction, moving away from affect that is emerging in the therapy. On the other hand, one must also monitor affect that leads to a breakthrough versus affect that threatens to overwhelm the delicate homeostatic balance.

We have suggested that the intrapsychic and the interpersonal are parts of a larger whole. By making a connection between the two in this case, we are illustrating that there is always a larger whole at play. The patient's character organization has heavily relied on expansive posturing for the majority of his working life, maintained by his position of power as CEO of his company. As he is losing his positional power, notice the symptomatic breakthrough in the form of dystonic nightmares, where loss of control, fears of being taken advantage of, and feelings of mistrust come to the surface. He now attempts to compensate for his loss by seeking assurance that his dreams are irrelevant to his true self. When the therapist does not provide this reassurance, notice how feelings of anger come to the surface.

When the therapist shifts from the inside to the outside and focuses on his wife and children, the therapist is attempting to create a bridge for the patient to utilize relational interaction in a less expansive and grandiose manner. However, the patient is not ready to confront his feelings of vulnerability more directly at this time.

Rather, the patient's response is, "I can't stand this feeling of being taken over." If we attempt to connect parts to a larger whole, the patient's response is telling us that the therapist's question is hitting too close for comfort. Given this response, what further questions and considerations come to mind regarding how to move forward clinically?

1. Are there any benefits to having the therapist "back off" and provide some form of reassurance to the patient?

2. What is the risk of the therapist being identified as someone else who wants to "take him over"?

3. What is the role of shame in this acute fear of being exposed?

4. Overall, what is the role of shame in this patient's character constellation?

Please refer to the Routledge website, Video 2.2: "Virginia"—Dismantling Perfectionistic Standards.

In the second video case example, we find a patient who has been in treatment for approximately two years. Early months of treatment were primarily dedicated to focusing on a. relationship issues where a breach of trust had occurred and b. helping the patient acquire clearer boundaries and expectations within the relationship moving forward. The therapy shifted its focus away from relational issues once the relationship had re-stabilized, and attention was directed toward the patient's perfectionistic standards around performance both for herself and others.

This session marks the beginning of emerging signs of the patient's ability to release the grip of rigidly held standards. Here we see how former standards of perfection are being questioned. We also see how these standards function as an overcompensation in an attempt to avoid deep-seated feelings of shame.

Patient: I want to go back to talking about my high standards for achievement, my need to be perfect. I think I'm making some progress on this.

Therapist: Yes, so tell me how you feel you've been doing with that.

Patient: I think that I'm letting go of that "super-high" bar I set for myself and for other people. But then I worry that the bar will swing too far the other way and I'll just let anything go and become a slug. I want to find a balance. (Laughs) I guess if I'm worried about that, maybe I haven't made as much progress reducing the bar after all.

Therapist: Tell me why you are worried that your standards will swing to the complete opposite side of the spectrum. Did something happen that causes you concern?

Patient: Well, yes, just the other day I was at a conference, and I spilled tomato juice all over my white pants—red tomato juice in my lap all over my pants. I never would have done that before.

Therapist: What do you mean? You never had an accident or spilled something before?

Patient: No, I didn't. Not that I can remember, anyway. I was always so careful. I didn't want to be sloppy. Now, I've made several stupid mistakes lately.

Therapist: What else happened?

Patient: Last weekend, I took a bunch of brush to the dump, and I was throwing it out of the back of the truck. I wasn't thinking, and as I stepped to throw a pile off the truck, I walked right off the flat bed and fell three feet. How could I be so stupid? I wasn't paying attention.

Therapist: That sounds pretty harsh, calling yourself stupid for something that was an accident.

Patient: Yes. But I never used to make those kinds of mistakes. I'm afraid that I'm not paying close enough attention anymore. See, that's why I'm afraid I'm going too far in the opposite direction.

Therapist: But it seems that you are also blaming and berating yourself if you let your guard down ever so slightly. This sounds a bit extreme—all or nothing—extreme high standards or fear of being a slug. You started to tell me that you were making some progress in lowering the super-high bar. Were there any examples that you felt good about this week when it came to slightly altering your expectations of yourself?

Patient: Well, yes, actually. When I spilled the tomato juice, I went into the bathroom, and there was another woman in the restroom. In the past I would have tried to hide so no one would ever see that I had made a mistake. But this time I said, "Look how stupid I was spilling tomato juice on my pants." I tried to make a joke about it.

Therapist: I see. So sharing the mistake made a difference?

Patient: Yes, I felt lighter. If I tell someone about it, it lessens it for me.

Therapist: Lessens what?

Patient: It lessens the shame I feel because *I'm* letting people know I'm not perfect. I told my secretary at work on Monday morning and my husband and son too.

Therapist: How does that lessen the shame?

Patient: Because when I told all of these people, they seemed to understand. Their reaction to me wasn't shaming, which initially was a surprise to me, by the way. But when I shared this, people started to tell me about *their* stupid things, the stupid things they did. It makes me feel like my mistake was more normal, like maybe I don't *have to be* perfect. And it makes it more real, too.

33

Therapist: Makes it more real?

Patient: In a funny way, it's a validation that I'm not a stupid person. What I *did* was stupid, but I'm not stupid. Does that make sense?

Analysis

In this case vignette, we see that the patient begins the session with an announcement of what appears to be a therapeutic gain. However, as is fairly typical, when the grip of an extreme standard begins to lessen, we see the patient articulate a fear that her behavior will swing completely in the opposite direction if she let's go, as evidenced by calling herself "stupid and sloppy."

This case example illustrates the back-and-forth tension between emerging authenticity and the more familiar defensively driven organizing schemas. This is often seen when a patient first becomes curious about *how* and *why* so much of her energy has been devoted to the need to be perfect. The therapeutic exchange represents a typical dialogic process that the therapist and patient often go through together. This process is in the service of gradually integrating split-off parts of the personality and thereby transmuting extreme standards into more workable realistic goals.

Questions for Discussion

1. How did you think the therapist handled the patient's fears around becoming sloppy and indifferent? Would you have said something different?

2. Discuss how the therapist wove the patient's view of mistakes into her belief about needing to be perfect.

3. What did you think about the timing of the therapist's remarks about directing the patient back to earlier "positive" changes that she had noticed when she had momentarily let go of the harsh, perfectionistic demands? Would you have done something differently?

---

4. *Explain your understanding of why the patient felt lighter once she told people about her mistake, rather than using her traditional posture of trying to hide it.*

5. *Discuss the patient's discovery process around differentiating between a "stupid behavior" and "being stupid."*

DYNAMIC FLUIDITY OF CHARACTER CHANGE

When an individual comes into treatment, our goal is to not only help reduce symptoms but to allow more of the real self to emerge. The following diagram may best illustrate our goal in terms of facilitating a change process. In the circle on the left, notice that the real self is hidden by layers of beliefs, behaviors, and symptoms that interfere with authentic emergence. As the therapy progresses, these interferences and defenses shrink in size, allowing more room for the real self to emerge.

The tension between the real self and the "invented" self is captured in Figure 2.1.

As you will notice from this diagram, the end result of a successful psychotherapy does not reflect the elimination of the character solution altogether. Memory traces of trauma and deprivation, with their attendant/reflexive response around triggers of disappointment and relational rupture, remain a part of the patient's historical narrative. Feelings of shame, isolation, and vulnerability run deep. Our goal in treatment is to increase the patient's resilience as the therapeutic attachment bond becomes more secure, allowing for the authentic self to occupy more psychic space.

PROCESS-ORIENTED ASSESSMENT: INTERSUBJECTIVE DYNAMIC CASE FORMULATION

The use of Dynamic Case Formulation as an assessment tool and roadmap for treatment has been with us for decades (Beck, 1975; Lazarus, 1981; Luborsky, 1984). Intersubjective Dynamic Case Formulation is a more recent theoretical method based on process-oriented, moment-to-moment tracking. This means that the therapist is guided by ever evolving relational exchanges,

Therapeutic Fluidity of Character Change

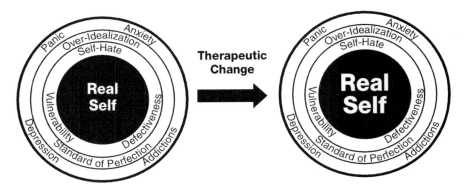

Figure 2.1 Therapeutic Fluidity of Character Change
Reprinted with permission from the book *Listening with Purpose: Entry Points into Shame and Narcissistic Vulnerability*, p. 22, J. Danielian & P. Gianotti, Lanham, Jason Aronson, 2012.

breakthroughs in treatment, and immersion into deeper affectively laden material.

- Intersubjective Dynamic Case Formulation involves advances in our understanding of two-person psychology. The therapist no longer sits as the "objective expert" but instead participates in the unfolding therapeutic relationship, with the relationship informing both assessment and intervention approaches.
- Using the perspective of a continually unfolding, dynamic case formulation is actually a process of immersion of oneself into the *other*. This approach answers the question of what's going on in the treatment at any given moment. The therapist relies on continuous feedback from the patient to modify therapeutic assessment as treatment progresses.
- In the past, Dynamic Case Formulations were based on assessment prior to full immersion into the treatment. Currently, Intersubjective Dynamic Case Formulation is an evolving ever-changing process that is based on reciprocal feedback between the patient and the therapist in all phases of the treatment.
- Thus, a more fully formulated assessment occurs where various parts of the whole picture are taken into account, including symptoms, intensity of affect, capacity for relational connection, rigidity of character defenses, over-determined efforts to maintain homeostasis *within* the psyche, as well as how one regulates and negotiates relational equilibrium.

Overall Questions for Review

1. How can deeper listening help us see genuine health in the context of non-health?

2. How would you begin to formulate a relationally based process-oriented (intersubjective) dynamic case formulation?

3. How might a patient's feelings of shame impact the course of therapy and the therapeutic relationship?

4. What factors might therapists need to keep in mind so as not to activate feelings of shame or other defensive reactions early on in the treatment?

In our final vignette example, we offer a summary of how the framework of character solutions can be used as a way of orienting our thinking and our listening in a way that is more compassionate and experience-near. Notice how the supervisory discussion marks shifts that can occur in how a patient is viewed once the therapist is able to see a character solution as mutable. Holding a framework of mutability around character allows for more compassion and less judgment, which in turn can generate a deeper sense of safety, one that yields hope and one that eventually will lead to a more optimistic outcome.

Please refer to the Routledge website, Video 2.3: Consultation Session on Character Solutions.

Discussion Questions

1. How would you describe the supervisee's shift around seeing characterological patterns as something fixed versus seeing these patterns as mutable?

   a. How does the supervisee articulate seeing the patient differently?

   b. How does the supervisee access within herself that would relationally create a potential shift in the therapist/patient dialogue and relationship?

2. How are character solutions an effort at adaptation?

   a. How does this change our ideas about "resistance"?

   b. How is health always present?

   c. How can the therapist reinforce health in the midst of seeing the character solution in action?

   d. How might the patient eventually begin to develop a self-reflective capacity with regard to tracking his/her own defensive triggers?

3. How does the framework of mutability and health contained within the "solution" potentially yield a more optimistic outcome to the treatment?

4. *How does the character solution, the "pseudo-solution," comprise aspects of the patient's best efforts, the best potential assets the person has?*

5. *Speak to the pseudo-solution as it contains elements of the authentic self that is trying to emerge.*

SUMMARY

Understanding the concept of character solutions is a key component in assessing, treating, and dismantling narcissistic defense structures. Overcompensations in the form of beliefs and behaviors are the foundational organizing principles behind the range of character "types," whether we are faced with the grandiose type, the deferring or placating type, or the distancing, dismissive type.

Differentiating between these *various types* and the *authentic self* is at the heart of therapeutic mirroring. This mirroring function will eventually allow aspects of resilience, curiosity, and determination to emerge (as we saw in the case example of Virginia).

How can one distinguish between the healthy real self and split-off parts of the self that *masquerade* as "the authentic person"? The following list provides examples of how the real self is made manifest in the world.

- The real self exhibits feelings of "wholeheartedness" and spontaneity.
- The real self is able to maintain a sense of mutuality in relationship with others.
- The real self listens to others' viewpoints with tolerance and respect.
- The real self builds on resilience and is on a path of ongoing growth throughout the life span.
- The real self recovers from disappointment without necessary retaliation.
- The real self holds a sense of vulnerability as something that is non-threatening, even positive.
- The real self is an inherent outcome of the individuation process, initially gained through secure attachments in childhood.

In this chapter, we have made connections to interpersonal neurobiology and attachment theory as they relate to the mutability of character structure, particularly the mutability of defensively constructed character solutions. When viewed through the lens of attachment, it is true that the development of a safe and secure therapeutic relationship becomes an important leverage in how the change process unfolds with individuals who struggle with narcissistic vulnerabilities. However, our work also *expands* upon on the contributions of neurological and attachment theories in several important ways.

First, the process of in-depth psychotherapy requires an overarching meta-theoretical framework that integrates intrapsychic, interpersonal, and contextual aspects of the psyche. Second, our attention to character organization in the context of the Four Quadrant Model is aimed at helping the therapist address the various components of the psyche simultaneously and in the present moment. Third, without the backdrop of character and the adaptive compensations that individuals develop to maintain homeostasis and their personal narrative, therapists may run the risk of missing important parts of the picture.

Our attention to character structure in the context of the Four Quadrant Model, as presented in the following chapters, helps the therapist see how the interconnected parts of the psyche connect to one another. Thus, *selfhood* becomes our integrating principle. Although self-development occurs within a relational container, how one's sense of self is shaped, constricted, traumatized, or encouraged to flourish is dependent on one's innate capacities and resilience, as well as the quality of one's attachments.

3

Immersion into Dynamic Listening

All psychoanalytic understanding is interpretive understanding, in the sense that it always entails a grasp of the meaning of something that has been expressed. This meaning belongs to an individual's personal subject world and becomes accessible to understanding in the medium of the analyst's empathy.

—Atwood and Stolorow (2014, p. 5)

The listening perspective from which the analyst works, however it evolves and is shaped by personal history, training, theory, and therapeutic experience, represents a sensibility that dramatically influences the course and nature of the analytic journey. . . . When the patient experiences us as a felt presence in his life, . . . it is the holistic feeling of intertwined connectedness that provides the necessary conditions for revitalizing thwarted development.

—Geist (2008, pp. 148–149)

A primary tool across all models of psychotherapy is editing and expanding the self-narrative of the left hemisphere to include the silent wisdom of the right.

—Cozolino (2012, p. 110)

Implicit in refining our listening skills is the goal of staying in the empathic posture of *presentness*. This posture has been labeled empathic immersion, and it is precisely how we sustain the mindfulness of focused attention. Directing our listening ear to the moment-to-moment present is how we achieve the solid ground of dynamic listening. Horney's observations on immersion into the patient's narrative are cogent. She states, "[An] aspect of wholehearted attention is unlimited receptivity. Work at those impressions that do sink in, with every way at your disposal . . . this kind of concentration of which I am speaking involves your feelings and is not just cold detached observation. Unlimited receptivity means being in it with all your feelings" (Horney, 1987, p. 20).

Stolorow, Brandchaft, and Atwood (1987) frame unlimited receptivity through a listening stance of *sustained empathic inquiry*. They state,

Sustained empathic inquiry by the analyst contributes to the formation of an intersubjective situation in which the patient increasingly comes to believe that his most profound emotional states and needs can be understood in depth. This, in turn, encourages the patient to develop and expand his own capacity for self-reflection and at the same time to persist in articulating ever more vulnerable and sequestered regions of his subjective life.

(pp. 10–11)

Dynamic listening also requires the ability to distinguish between left brain interactions, which include interventions such as therapist interpretation and cognitive-behavioral strategies, and right brain interactions, which address injuries to one's sense of self and difficulties forming secure relational attachments. Schore and Schore (2012) identify key components of effective psychotherapy that are directed at tuning into and improving the integration of right brain capacities. These include empathy, the regulation of affect, the ability to receive and express non-verbal communication, the sensitivity to register slight changes in expression and emotion, and the awareness of one's own subjective and intersubjective experience.

Neurological findings have confirmed what experience-near practitioners have known for some time. That is, empathy and attending to the nuance of verbal as well as non-verbal cues enable the practitioner to create a therapeutic holding environment that is reparative. However, this holding environment requires a quality of listening attention that is tuned in to ruptures of attunement and shame sensitivity.

Overall, our experience has demonstrated that listening has suffered from under-attention in the listening professions. This is a hardship because listening cannot be achieved by a simple recognition of its importance on an abstract or intellectual level. It is through the posture of immersion that we become more aware of deeper listening skills that develop into a systemic understanding of the component parts of a complex picture of the psyche. This involves:

- Sensitization to over-determined efforts at character solutions that maintain a homeostatic, yet precarious, balance within the patient.
- Attunement to deeply buried feelings of shame and self-hate that drive the defensive constructs.
- Attunement to hidden sources of strength and resilience.

Empathic presentness allows us to simultaneously experience the mechanisms of dissociative splitting and its compulsively driven need to prove one's value and self-worth. It should be noted, however, that the components of narcissistic injury are not "static states." A more compassionate understanding of narcissism sees this inner struggle as an attempt at self-protection.

As such, narcissistic injury is best conceptualized and visually captured on a continuum of defenses. These defenses are, as we have mentioned, fluid and subject to change based on context and the therapeutic relationship.

The following diagram illustrates the continuum of narcissistic vulnerability.

Continuum of Narcissistic Vulnerability

Diagnosed   Degrees   Optimal
Narcissism   of Injury   Health

Figure 3.1 Continuum of Narcissistic Vulnerability

Grounding ourselves in attachment theory, one must consider that a person's discomfort around the experience of personal vulnerability stems from some degree of failure with early attachment figures. This raises the question, "Who had a 'perfect' childhood?" Because we all carry some measure of less-than-optimal attachment experiences, attention to the continuum of vulnerability applies to the therapist as well as the patient. In a relational model, this means attending to our patients' areas of vulnerability as well as being mindful of what vulnerabilities may be triggered in *us*, or some combination of the two in the intersubjective present.

In a "two-person" model of therapeutic interaction, the intersubjective stance shifts the therapist away from "objective" observer and acknowledges the complexity and subjectivity of therapeutic listening. Therefore, how we hold a sense of the vulnerability of all people becomes a critical ingredient to compassionate and thoughtful listening.

We have stressed that in each stage of therapy, it is the therapist's task to listen for areas of vulnerability *and* signs of emerging health. Holding this dialectic tension between defensive-driven homeostasis and emerging signs of health and growth becomes an important part of the listening task.

LISTENING FOR DEGREES OF OVERCOMPENSATION

Our way of conceptualizing how the (defensively driven) homeostatic mechanisms present themselves is illustrated in the diagram below.

This diagram of the three-legged stool allows us to visually comprehend the interconnected relationship that comprises the character solution. Each leg of the stool represents an aspect of a complex and interconnecting defense pattern, one that manifests within the patient's interpersonal relationships, through emotional distancing or through rigidly held beliefs and performance expectations for self and for others. The interconnectivity of these components represents a patient's attempts at creating psychic homeostatic balance. During the course of therapy, the therapist's task as much as possible is to stay connected

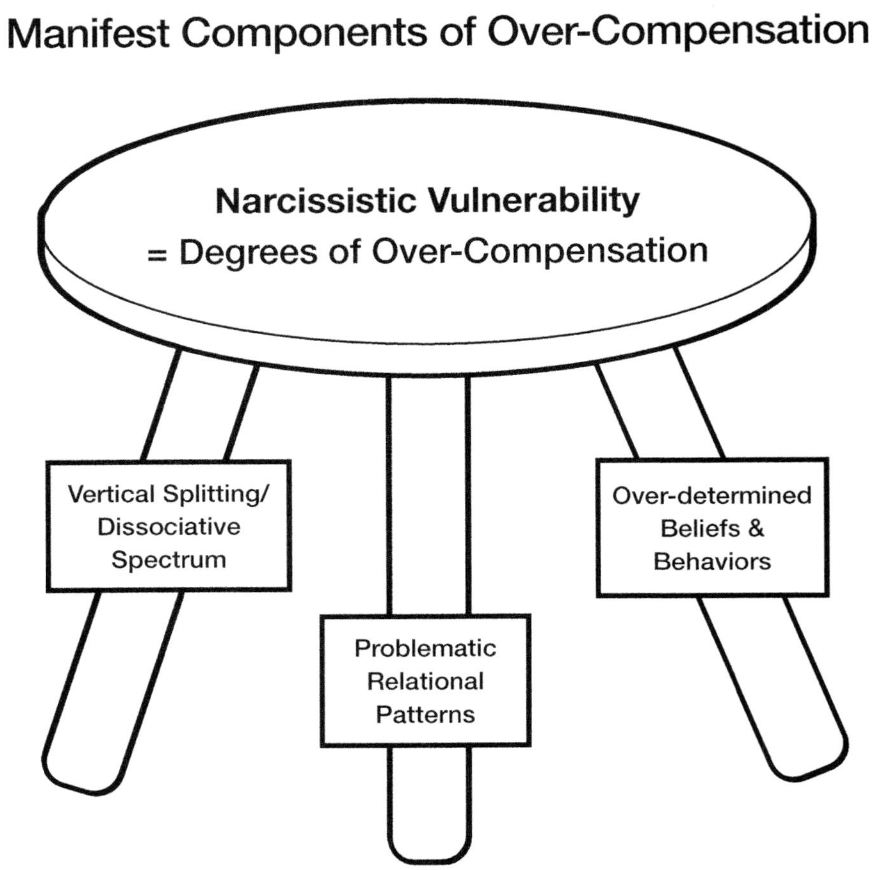

Manifest Components of Over-Compensation

Figure 3.2 Manifest Components of Overcompensation

to each of these dimensions simultaneously. In addition, the therapist listens for the *pervasiveness* of defensiveness along any of the dimensions illustrated. High degrees of rigidity indicate the measure of fragility within the core personality and character structure.

For further clarification, each of the three legs of the stool is elaborated as follows:

- **Vertical splitting—as determined by the depth to which dissociation is triggered to help reduce internal conflict.** To assess the degree of narcissistic vulnerability, the therapist looks for how integrated the *affective* component of a patient's narrative is with the *cognitive* component of self-observation (or recalled memory). One might ask:

  a. Are emotions completely disavowed or treated with contempt?

   b. Does affective material flood the clinical narrative to the point of momentary disorganization or fragmentation?

   c. Does the patient contradict his or her own statements or beliefs within a session?

   d. Is there a flattening of affect around certain triggers?

- **Over-determined beliefs & behaviors—as determined by how absolute or compulsively driven they are.** In assessing the degree of compulsivity in a patient's beliefs and behaviors, the therapist looks for the amount of flexibility or adaptability within a patient's repertoire, especially when unexpected circumstances present themselves.

  a. To what degree can the patient exhibit curiosity around identified beliefs and behaviors that comprise the compulsively created solution?

  b. Are the patient's beliefs rigidly upheld in an "all-or-nothing" construction, or is the patient capable of tolerating differences of opinion?

  c. Is the patient capable of pausing and reflecting before voicing opinions or moving to action?

  d. Does the patient exhibit a "fatalistic" attitude toward life that inhibits spontaneity and optimism?

- **Problematic relational patterns—as determined by the degree to which the patient is able to maintain mutuality, fairness, and honesty within a relationship.** In assessing *relationship* health, the therapist looks for the quality of relational expectations, including how the individual handles disappointments in the relational sphere.

  a. Does the patient hold the same standards or expectations for himself as he does for others, or is there a double standard at play?

  b. When another person needs the patient's emotional support, is he able to provide empathy, or is he quick to express impatience or rapid solutions?

  c. Does the patient retaliate when disappointed, or is she able to express needs and disappointments directly?

  d. Does the patient create tests where others either pass or fail?

The above graphic offers a way of conceptualizing crucial areas of therapeutic listening. The diagram covers the degree of dissociative splitting that is required to reduce internal conflict; the degree of rigidity or flexibility of the patient's organizing schemas around beliefs, goals, and behaviors; and the capacity for mutuality in relationships that the patient is able to demonstrate. By shifting between these areas of attention, the therapist becomes more adept at attending to any leg of the stool.

Greater attunement occurs in the immediate present as the listening process deepens. When the therapist is able to navigate more freely through these components of "listening attention," she or he will eventually be able to identify not only what is being actively expressed but also what is kept hidden from view. What is omitted from the dialogue is as important as what the patient focuses on, and systemic attention to both allows the therapist to become more attuned to how the parts (both hidden and revealed) fit into the larger whole of psychic organization.

If the therapist observes that a patient abruptly shifts away from affectively charged material, there is a high likelihood that a micro-dissociation has occurred. Tracking what content preceded the dissociation is critical in determining how the parts fit or do not fit into an integrated narrative. For example, did the patient experience a micro-dissociation when the dialogue is focused in the relational sphere, or did the dissociative trigger occur when the patient began discussing and defending his or her beliefs or behaviors? This is how the visual illustration of the three-legged stool becomes important for assessment and analysis.

A further example illustrating the utility of the three-legged stool would be to have the therapist track inconsistencies in the patient's internally held standards for *self* and compare them to the standards and expectations the patient holds for *others*. This level of assessment tracks:

- The level of expectation.
- The pressure placed on self or others in hopes that expectations are fulfilled.
- The degree of disappointment if expectations are not met.

Together, these become valuable indices in assessing the rigidity of the splits defending against narcissistic vulnerabilities.

Our discussion is meant to be a helpful construction of attending to multiple dimensions of the therapeutic exchange as it unfolds. Empathic immersion into the various dimensions of dynamic process is much like "tuning into a radio frequency." All radio waves exist within the atmosphere. Tuning into the proper frequency allows us to hear something new or understand how parts fit together in a new way. This ever-changing, unfolding process of formulation can keep the therapist attuned and flexible, and able to modify assumptions as the treatment progresses.

Application: A Clinical Questionnaire

Think about a case you have treated, one that was difficult or challenging. As you recall areas of difficulty or a sense of relational disconnection in the dialogue, analyze whether the rupture occurred more frequently around one leg of the stool than others.

1. What might you do differently in terms of dialogic inquiry to gain more information about what is being triggered?

---

2. *Give yourself* permission to be confused *when a rupture occurs within a session. Pause and go back to the moment of confusion. Become curious with your patient about "what just happened." Write down three different ways of inviting the patient to become curious with you in the present moment. Here are three examples to help get you started. Fill in your own examples, using your own language and style.*

    a. *"Could we pause for a minute before moving on? I'm wondering why you shifted from talking about your disappointment with John to chastising yourself for not doing more to fix the situation."*

    b. *"You seem to have drifted off for a moment. What just happened there?"*

    c. *"I'm sorry. I'm not following you. Could you explain how you arrived at that conclusion so I can learn more about how you thought through your decision?"*

    d.

    e.

    f.

3. *Identify areas of repeated exchanges or patterns of exchange with a patient where you become slightly uncomfortable. Try to identify the specific trigger around your own discomfort.*

a. *Is the patient articulating a hidden expectation of you around the treatment process?*

b. *Is the patient exhibiting impatience?*

c. *Are you sensing an area of rigidity that seems too "hot to handle"?*

d. *Is negative transference beginning to emerge?*

Note: *The questions listed above would be useful to complete as a solo exercise, or they can be used as a springboard for discussion with a colleague in peer supervision. Practicing various options for how you might momentarily "stop" the therapeutic dialogue is one way to slow the process down and gather information that may be hidden from view. The greater the comfort the therapist has in finding phrases to help slow the process down, the deeper the listening exchange will become.*

Video Case Vignettes

In the following section, three video case vignettes are provided to demonstrate how to *listen for and navigate* verbal content that highlights all *three* legs of the stool. Notice how quickly shifts in the dialogue may occur, as the patient moves from one leg of the stool to the other.

Please refer to the Routledge website, Video 3.1: Three Legs of a Clinical Stool.

The first case vignette illustrates how the therapist is able to move around the three legs of the stool while tracking moments where the patient dissociates from material during the treatment exchange.

Patient: I just showed our summer house to a couple from NYC. My husband doesn't want to sell, was rude during the showing, but they're still interested. I know this because I took the call last night

	without telling Larry. This feels like a door opened for me. Isn't this exciting?
Therapist:	It feels like a door opened for you?
Patient:	It's buying my freedom back.
Therapist:	It's buying your freedom back, in what way?
Patient:	If we sell the house, I can move. I'll finally have my freedom from Larry.
Therapist:	I see. Have you spoken about this with him?
Patient:	Well, no. I was waiting until I had some leverage.
Therapist:	And the leverage is having the money from the house sale?
Patient:	Yes.
Therapist:	And you don't have leverage now? Don't you both have quite a bit of money in the bank?
Patient:	Well, yes. But I've been afraid to bring it up.
Therapist:	And what would be different if you sold the summer house? How does that give you leverage?
Patient:	I could talk to him then. Maybe he would be reasonable.
Therapist:	So, you are hoping that the house sale will make it easier for you to have a difficult conversation?
Patient:	Yes, I could just appeal to his reason.
Therapist:	What would be different about this situation with the house sale that gives you hope that he would be reasonable?
Patient:	(Looks confused, starts to stare off into space) I'm sorry, what did you say?
Therapist:	I asked what you hoped would be different about this situation.
Patient:	I guess having the money would make it easier.
Therapist:	How so?
Patient:	I don't know. That he would have something to hold onto, and so would I. (Looks down) Something to give me the courage to speak up.
Therapist:	Having the money would give you the courage to speak?
Patient:	(Looks off to the right) What? I'm sorry. I'm having a hard time concentrating on what you're saying. What did you say? (Pause) I'm avoiding something, aren't I?
Therapist:	Well, we don't have to rush anything. We can take our time. I know it's hard. Whatever needs to come out will come out when it's time.
Patient:	Thank you, I just want to catch my breath. It's about my husband and me, isn't it? It's always about that.
Therapist:	It seems as though there is something about the way we are talking about you and Larry that is making you uncomfortable. Let's slow it down a little bit. Nothing has to be decided in this moment. How

	you're feeling right now, in the room? Is this what happens when you try to speak to Larry?
Patient:	Yes, it's as if I disappear. I get so frightened when it comes to making any kind of move. I even get frightened by the idea of making a move.
Therapist:	And yet, you are miserable at home, aren't you?
Patient:	(Looks down, begins to cry) Yes, yes. It's awful. It feels like I become frozen; then, it's as if I lose the sense of (pause) me.
Therapist:	Yes, you want to leave because you don't feel safe, and you can't leave because it doesn't feel safe.
Patient:	(Looks up) That's it exactly. (Pause) I guess. But, it doesn't make any sense.

Questions for Discussion

1. Describe where you see the three legs of the stool being activated in the sequence.

2. Where are the places within the dialogue that the patient begins to dissociate?

3. Discuss the therapist's timing of shifting from the patient's fear of making a move to the reality of being miserable at home.

   a. What else might we have learned if the therapist inquired further into the feelings of fear and "not being able to make a move"?

   b. What might be the benefits and downsides of shifting back to the reality of her misery at this point in the case vignette?

4. Could the therapist have done something further when the patient went back to trying to talk about the feeling of "being frozen"?

5. Discuss the merits of the therapist pointing out the patient's double bind at the end of this sequence.

   a. Why do you think the patient showed signs of relief?

   b. How is the power of naming an internal conflict or double bind helpful in initiating the patient's eventual capacity for self-reflection?

In the following case vignette, notice how the therapist tracks, moment-to-moment, the shifts in the patient dialogue and affect. Also notice how the over-determined efforts on the part of the patient are manifesting in an attempt to maintain an emotional homeostatic balance. And note how the therapist handles the patient's irritation with her husband.

Please refer to the Routledge website, Video 3.2: Deflated Expectations.

Questions for Discussion

1. How might you explain the patient's irritation once her husband granted her wish for a vacation home?

   a. What clarifying questions might you ask around her rapid shifts in affect between initially feeling nothing to feeling deflated, empty, and uncomfortable?

    b. How does shutting down and feeling "nothing" maintain the narcissistic homeostatic balance?

2. *What function does the patient becoming irritated with her husband have in terms of her capacity for affect-regulation?*

3. *How would you describe the therapist's efforts in trying to direct the patient back to her own internal feeling state?*

    a. In terms of timing?

    b. In terms of tracking?

    c. In terms of planting a seed with regard to increasing her conscious awareness of affective shifts that occur internally?

4. *How would you explain the patient's last comment about noticing her response as "a little strange"?*

    a. Describe what the therapist was trying to do in this moment?

    b. What do you think might have happened if the therapist did not provide reassurance?

5. *What hints do you have that the patient carries unarticulated expectations of the therapist?*

In the last clinical vignette, we offer a case consultation around a couple's therapy. Notice how the episodes of affect dysregulation shift between husband and wife. Each member of the marriage feels under-appreciated. Neither seems very interested in making moves to change. Rather, there is a wish to have the other person change.

Please refer to the Routledge website, Video 3.3: Consultation Session on Tracking the Three Legs of the Stool.

Questions for Review

1. *What would you have done when both members of the marriage said that they weren't interested in change?*

2. *Patricia asks the supervisee if he noted the inconsistency between the husband's report of being passive and then yelling at their son. Why would it be important to stop and get clarification at this point in terms of:*

   a. *A possible split around self-perception and behavior?*

   b. *Slowing the process down?*

   c. *Getting a clearer picture around affect-regulation and affective triggers?*

3. *Notice that the supervisee is feeling a great deal of pressure around the multiple needs of the family. How is the supervisee getting ahead of himself?*

---

4. *Notice that Patricia goes back to the prior session and focuses on each of the members of the couple stating that they were not interested in changing.*

   a. *How does repeating the patient's comment slow the process down and draw attention to the patient's expectations around her own efforts?*

   b. *Why does the therapist follow-up this statement with the question, "What were you hoping for by coming into therapy?"*

5. *Notice that the supervisee made an assumption rather than getting verbal clarification around the patient's expectations. What is the danger in leaping to a conclusion as to a possible motivation for coming into treatment?*

6. *Focusing on what's not being said around patient expectations of the therapy allows for hope to remain secret with the potential to later erupt as a negative transference disappointment. Discuss why formulating a clear contract with a patient up front is critically important.*

SUMMARY

In this chapter, we have presented a number of experience-near issues relevant to deeper immersion into empathic listening. We have stressed the role of moment-to-moment listening and processing as a vehicle to help the therapist track parts of a complex, systemic whole. In addition we have encouraged therapists to conceptualize the complexity of understanding narcissistic injury from a non-pathological vantage point. If narcissism is viewed as a set of protective mechanisms that have been put in place in an attempt to compensate for feelings of vulnerability or unworthiness, greater compassion and immersion are possible.

Narcissistic mechanisms were presented on a continuum of severity and included possible triggers to our own vulnerabilities. Assessment of severity of narcissistic injury involves an understanding of the dissociative process, including the identification of micro-dissociations. In addition, a thorough assessment must include a systemic and holistic understanding of the intrapsychic and interpersonal dimensions of the self.

Although the components of attending to these various aspects of therapeutic assessment and process are described sequentially, this by no way is meant to convey that immersion into deeper degrees of listening is a linear process. It is merely an unfortunate limitation of trying to describe a multi-faceted process through the medium of the printed page. In reality, all of the components of the listening process are interconnected to each other in an acausal, non-linear, and circular fashion.

Neither psychic reality nor, as we are discovering, the brain itself is organized along linear, fixed lines. The deeper we empathically probe and the better we are able to listen, the more the process embraces ever-widening circles of psychic reality.

The diagram of the three-legged stool was designed as a visual reference to help the therapist tune in to the multi-layered components of dynamic listening. By separating these processes into organizing schemas that span the affective, cognitive, and relational components of psychic organization, the therapist is better able to see areas of connection and disconnection within the various parts. Again, these three dimensions of psychic organization represent patient attempts at creating a homeostatic balance and keeping shame at bay.

For ease of reading we have listed these dimensions as follows:

- By attending to possible dissociative processes that may be triggered within the session, the therapist is better able to monitor and assess the degree of affect-regulation or dysregulation and amount of effort required to maintain this sense of equilibrium.
- By monitoring over-determined beliefs and behaviors, the therapist is able to track and measure the degree of patients' rigidity of thought processes including the degree of compulsivity and effort required to "prove" one's superiority to others.
- By acquiring a history of patients' relational patterns, hopes, expectations, and attendant behaviors, the therapist can assess the quality of attachment and attachment style, the level of capacity for mutuality and fairness, the degree of self-sacrifice *demanded* to maintain a relationship, and the level of disequilibrium that occurs when disappointments around expectations of self and others occur.

Each of these aspects of the intrapsychic and relational components that comprise the relational container of the therapeutic relationship requires continual monitoring and attending. Represented as parts of a three-legged stool of overcompensation, they also act as an introduction to our Four Quadrant Model, which will be covered in the next chapter.

55

4

The Four Quadrant Model

Danielian and Gianotti call their model experience-near because they don't intend it to be a diagnostic tool or a guide to technique. They suggest we simply hold all four quadrants in mind in order to listen to patients more deeply in the moment. When we can hear the splits hidden in what they say, our experience-near responses will subtly communicate what we hear. Bit by bit and roaming all over the quadrants with us, clients will come to experience the workings of their own personal solution to the problem of shamed vulnerability.

—Patricia A. DeYoung (2015, p. 147)

We begin with an in-depth review of the Four Quadrant Model. The model is best understood as a diagram or a process grid, one that is fluid and circular in nature, as opposed to presenting a picture of the personality that is linear or fixed. Each quadrant is part of a whole, and the model draws our attention to how the various parts of the psyche connect and form a stressful but homeostatic balance.

The model also represents a picture of varying degrees of narcissistic injury. Depending on the patient's level of rigidity, the therapist can assess how mechanisms of overcompensation (displayed both within and between each quadrant) function in concert to maintain an over-determined homeostatic balance. In addition, the therapist can use the model to highlight how protective mechanisms are used to keep feelings of shame outside of conscious awareness. The utility of the grid is to provide the therapist with a tracking system that connects the parts (each of the four quadrants) to other parts and to an ever-evolving characterological whole.

THE NON-LINEARITY OF THE QUADRANTS—HOW TO USE THE MODEL

- Although this graphic is designed in quadrant form, the model is intended to capture a dynamic picture of a systemic, intrapsychic, and relational whole.
- Since this is a systemic grid, activation in any of the quadrants can occur at any time and can move in any direction, in any combination, and without regard to linearity.

The Four Quadrant Model

CONSCIOUS

QUADRANT ONE

How I View Myself

ASPIRATIONS
Conscious wishes and ambitions, drive for perfection, need for acknowledgement and continuing praise for accomplishments

BELIEF SYSTEMS
Over-invested syntonic absolutes, self-righteous superiority, prideful intolerance

SELF-IMPOSED STANDARDS
Over-determined moral or intellectual standards, inflation or deflation of one's efforts & contributions

QUADRANT TWO

Symptoms

DEPRESSIVE CLUSTER
Ranging from dysthymia to hopelessness and despair

BEHAVIORAL CLUSTER
Exhaustion, deprivation, lack of self-care

ANXIETY CLUSTER
Confusion, inertia, paralysis, fear of emptiness

SOMATIC CLUSTER
Addictions, body dysmorphia, eating disorders

SYNTONIC

DYSTONIC

SHAME

QUADRANT THREE

Loyal Waiting

♦ For the "perfect" idealized other
♦ For fantastical wishes for happiness or salvation
♦ For outside recognition of the purity of one's own self-sacrifice
♦ Wish for absolute answers, assurances, guarantees
♦ Rescue from pain & suffering
♦ A confusion between hidden, grandiose wishes and the real self

QUADRANT FOUR

Revenge Enactments

♦ Grossly self-damaging behaviors ranging from neglect to suicidal acts
♦ Wish to harm others, ranging from devaluation to acts of violence
♦ Sabotage of success (self or other)
♦ Repeated testing/demands of proof
♦ Self-hate due to disillusionment or humiliation
♦ Externalization of blame

DISSOCIATIVE SPECTRUM: CONSCIOUS, BUT HIDDEN / PRECONSCIOUS / UNCONSCIOUS

Figure 4.1 The Four Quadrant Model
Reprinted with permission from the book *Listening with Purpose: Entry Points into Shame and Narcissistic Vulnerability* (p. 37), J. Danielian & P. Gianotti, Lanham, Jason Aronson, 2012.

- The patient's persistent over-reliance on a particular quadrant can telegraph to the therapist that other quadrants (other aspects of the psyche) may be kept hidden from view.

- Treatment must include an understanding of character formation, identified as organizing schemas that heavily shape persistent patterns of beliefs, standards, and expectations of self and others.
- How a patient engages in the activation or denial of a quadrant gives us an understanding of how the various parts of the psyche fit or don't fit into an authentically integrated and evolving whole.
- The avoidance of any given quadrant is precisely what allows us to begin to listen for what is being said and what is not being said. It also helps us recognize how compulsively driven character solutions are organized.

A detailed explanation of each of the four quadrants follows. Elaboration on each of the quadrants will be accompanied by video case examples that illustrate how the content of a particular quadrant manifests within the therapeutic dialogue. As we begin, we draw your attention to the center of the diagram. You will notice that shame connects all four quadrants. From the perspective of narcissistic injury, shame represents the driving force behind overcompensated character solutions. Therefore, how one views the self, how one holds expectations in relation to others, and how one handles disappointments both internally and with others, all become part of the reenactment of the narcissistic character solution.

From the perspective of narcissistic injury, the association to vulnerability is not a neutral experience. Vulnerability triggers memories of fragility, defectiveness, lack of safety, even terror. For individuals with insecure attachment histories, others are not to be trusted; caregivers (and therefore all others in the present) are met with a certain degree of underlying mistrust. At the core of the injured self is a deeply buried or consciously hidden memory of inadequacy and mistrust of the world. Compensatory efforts to create a cohered self are the patient's attempts to bypass any encounter with his or her own vulnerability as well as bypassing any need for reliance on or feedback from others.

A REVIEW OF EACH QUADRANT WITH ACCOMPANYING CASE EXAMPLES

Quadrant One Is a Depiction of "Who I Am" and "What I Find 'Congruent' in Myself"

It highlights:

- The degree to which the patient is defensively driven toward idealized aims.
- The level of attachment the patient holds to over-determined standards of perfectionism.

Quadrant One

How I View Myself

ASPIRATIONS

Conscious wishes and ambitions, drive for perfection, need for
acknowledgement and continuing praise for accomplishments

BELIEF SYSTEMS

Over-invested syntonic absolutes,
self-righteous superiority, prideful intolerance

SELF-IMPOSED STANDARDS

Over-determined moral or intellectual standards, inflation
or deflation of one's efforts & contributions

Figure 4.2 Quadrant One
Reprinted with permission from the book *Listening with Purpose: Entry Points into Shame and Narcissistic Vulnerability*, (p. 41), J. Danielian & P. Gianotti, Lanham, Jason Aronson, 2012.

- The degree of absolute thinking with regard to beliefs (the need to be "right," the capacity to tolerate differences of opinion).
- The degree of inflation or deflation of the patient's own efforts.

Quadrant One also contains genuine aspects of the real self. These authentic components of the personality are often hidden underneath feelings of shame and inadequacy, which have driven the compulsive solutions. It is important for the therapist to remember that authentic components still remain accessible, since genuine aspects of the personality are often hidden or held hostage by rigidly held efforts to prove self-worth.

Since these healthy and unhealthy forces are continually in conflict, tensions are inherent and bring into being mechanisms of dissociation and reduced consciousness. Hence, the character structure is constantly negotiating between health and non-health. Conversely, healthy currents of needs, hopes, aspirations, or wishes can *carry* undercurrents of perfectionistic demands and other owned and disowned absolutes that affect the person both intrapsychically and interpersonally. These absolutes are, of course, themselves compulsively driven and over-idealized. The Four Quadrant Model, therefore, creates a pictorial representation of these conflicting tensions between the real self and defensive mechanisms driving the dissociative process.

Since perfection is not possible, what is *inflated* becomes readily *deflated*, leading the patient to easily feel exhausted, depleted, hopeless, or shamed. This is why compulsively driven solutions that attempt to "puff up" the personality create psychic fragility. These defensively driven efforts are unsustainable in the long run because life is inevitably filled with disappointments, disagreements, or thwarted healthy ambitions.

Video Case Vignette Illustrating Quadrant One

Please refer to the Routledge website, Video 4.1: Disorganized Attachment and Overcompensation.

In the following case illustration, you will see how over-determined efforts to maintain a sense of value and stability are created. The patient is able to explain to the therapist how she uses her innate talents and competence to escape a family system with a disorganized attachment style. In this instance, the patient is able to employ over-determined efforts to escape the chaotic family system, but she is unable to access her authentic self in the service of letting go of this learned pattern of relating. In this session, however, we are able to see early signs of a breakthrough as evidenced by the patient's increased self-reflective capacities as well as her ability to access feelings of anger toward both caregivers.

Patient:	I've been thinking a lot about what we were talking about regarding my over-doing when I was visiting my daughter. I pondered the "why" of it all last week. I think it has to do with issues of my value as a mother, my insecurities, I mean. There are aspects of me trying to be superwoman.
Therapist:	What does the word superwoman mean to you?
Patient:	It means that I can do more, hold more projects together, handle more than anyone else. (Pause) I can also see how this connects to me as a child. It was my attempt to get noticed and appreciated. I never felt appreciated or cared for, so I learned early on to try to help my mother out. As the oldest, I took the running of the household onto my shoulders—to try to manage the chaos and to take care of my younger siblings. (Pause) But, as a child, I never felt competent enough.
Therapist:	You remember having that feeling?
Patient:	Things kept going wrong. My parents never fixed anything. We never had enough food in the house, or the food had gone bad in

the refrigerator. We were expected to eat it anyway, and if anyone tried to complain, we got accused of not being grateful. (Shakes her head) It was a crazy house. All I wanted to do was get out. (Pause) Then, as an adult, when I finally did get out, I realized I could gain more mastery of the world. I worked really hard and got a lot of attention. People were impressed by how much I could pull off. It was a short-term high, like a drug that made me feel on top of the world—free. I could say to myself, "Ok, aren't I great!" (Pause) It was also a defense and protection against just showing up with my normal strengths and weaknesses—feeling however I felt or being just normal me in the moment.

Therapist: Because being in the moment is risky?

Patient: More vulnerable. I would be more open to criticism.

Therapist: So, you carry an internal expectation that others out there will criticize?

Patient: Yeah, and they won't want me.

Therapist: So, the only way people will want you is if you're proving yourself somehow?

Patient: (Tears up) Yeah, yeah. I think it goes back to childhood. As children, we were made to feel burdens to our parents, especially Dad.

Therapist: How did you know you were a burden to your dad?

Patient: His constant frustration with us. "You broke that." And his emotional despair. He was in constant fear that we had broken something.

Therapist: The example you gave me didn't sound like despair. It sounded like anger or frustration.

Patient: Oh, he was disappointed, but he'd say, "It's broken. We'll never get another like it." Anger I could deal with. Anger was easier than the guilt he made us feel. And that goes to a huge paradigm for me—being trapped into a no-win situation.

Therapist: What do you mean?

Patient: We were constantly being set up as kids. The toilets didn't work, the electricity didn't work, things were broken that we didn't break, but we were constantly being blamed. "Why did you break this lamp?" But the lamp had been broken for years. There was some wiring problem. It was like that with everything. (Pause) It was a home filled with layers of fear. The fear was always there; we were always waiting for something to happen—to be blamed for something. (Looks up) I remember this time when my father was driving us to school, and the muffler on our car was broken. He hadn't gotten it fixed for months. But when we were coming up to the school and had to go past the crossing guard, he would say to us, "Stop making so much noise in the back seat. You're making so much noise that she may stop us, and then it will be your fault that Dad has to go to jail." My life story was being trapped, the constant fear of being trapped, some big authority figure would trap me.

Therapist: So, your efforts to become superwoman was your way of getting out of the trap?

Patient: And stay out of it. To stay out of controlling and trapping men. Strong women don't seem to scare me. Weak women scare me. I guess it's because they remind me of my mother. But, what I can't understand is why I keep being drawn to strong, controlling men. Maybe I'm drawn to sado-masochistic relationships. Is there something really wrong with me?

Therapist: What made you call yourself masochistic?

Patient: Well, we talked about this pattern a lot in my prior therapy. But that never felt right to me. I don't think I'm masochistic. I hate the feeling of being trapped.

Therapist: Yes, nobody really likes to feel pain and suffer. And I don't think it's fair to blame you for the mistreatment of others. That sounds too much like what your father did to you, trying to make you feel guilty to avoid looking at his own behavior.

Patient: (Looks up with astonished look on her face) Thank you. Thank you. Nobody ever saw this part of my father. He always presented a reasonable front. Self-sacrificing father with a mentally ill wife and five children. I think he stayed up at night trying to trap us in situations where we had to suffer or live in fear. That son of a bitch.

Questions for Discussion

1. *What effect did the therapist's questions around understanding the patient's over-determined efforts in Quadrant One have in terms of revealing the patient's overall dilemma with both of her caregivers?*

2. *How do you understand the patient's sense of "pride" in trying to achieve superwoman status?*

a. How was the patient rewarded in childhood for her attempts to be more than a child, in fact, to be her mother's helper and eventually superwoman?

b. What insights does the patient currently exhibit in terms of her ability to track the over-determined stance of Quadrant One?

3. Why do you think that the therapist continued to refer to Quadrant One by using the phrase "superwoman"?

4. How do you understand the breakthrough of anger at the end of this video segment?

Please refer to the Routledge website, Video 2.2: "Virginia"—Dismantling Perfectionistic Standards.

In the following case illustration of Quadrant One, we direct you to a video initially presented in Chapter 2. We refer to this case now to highlight how character solutions and their over-determined efforts become quite manifest in the Four Quadrant Model. Whereas our first case example illustrating Quadrant One revealed anger under the surface, this case highlights how the therapist works with releasing the grip of perfectionistic standards. She does so by connecting behavioral overcompensations to the patient's attempts to avoid feelings of shame.

Video Case Analysis

In the beginning of this case vignette, the patient announces that she is making progress around lessening her high standards of perfection. However, she follows this with a worry that she will swing too far in the opposite direction and become sloppy. This is a fairly typical reaction when patients begin to show signs of letting go of harsh standards. The polar opposite presents itself—from perfect to sloppy—or not caring at all.

Notice that the therapist follows this admission of fear with a question that is anchored to a behavior, wondering if something specific had happened that supported the patient's concern. In directing the dialogue to a specific behavioral incident, the therapist is able to get more information about both the patient's fears as well as what comprises the basis for the all-or-nothing thinking. Important information is then revealed about accidents being mistakes, and mistakes aren't supposed to happen if you are vigilant and careful. In this organizing schema around the need to be perfect, mistakes become the evidence of failure. Internalized, hidden shame is exposed through the mistake, thus the need for increased hyper-vigilance. This case example illustrates how the vicious cycle of shame is self-reinforcing.

Questions for Review

1. *Why do you think that the therapist shifted the conversation away from the patient's self-blame to how the patient felt good about letting go of perfectionistic standards? Would you have done something differently? If so, what would you have done next?*

2. *Why do you think that sharing "something stupid" with a stranger made a difference in loosening the grip of her perfectionistic standards?*

3. *How is this sharing directly connected to loosening the grip of shame?*

Summary of Quadrant One

Patients often seek therapy at the point when the over-determined solutions around proving self-worth are met with disappointment, especially as these efforts require more and more energy to maintain. Our task as therapists is not to create further deflation, since the therapeutic process itself engages this disillusionment over time. Rather, our goal is to find ways to support and nourish nascent health until the patient can begin to confront his or her heretofore self-sustaining illusions.

We work to be able to recognize the *difference* between healthy goals, ambitions, and esteem versus an over-inflated, grandiose sense of self. The key barometer here is to listen for the distinction between what is presented as the character solution as opposed to the emergence of the real self.

The therapeutic tasks associated with Quadrant One are summarized as follows:

- Is the patient's self-image or personal ambition grounded in reality?
- Does the patient need to inflate his or her accomplishments at the expense of others?
- Does the patient allow for differing beliefs or opinions?
- Is the patient able to admit mistakes and apologize without self-or-other recrimination?
- What is the degree of rigidity or flexibility in thinking, goals, and beliefs?
- Does the patient hold different standards for self as opposed to others?
- Does the patient exhibit any signs of hopefulness or self-compassion around the possibility of change?
- Is the patient filled with feelings of despair, fear, and self-loathing when change might become possible?

The above questions focusing on Quadrant One help us to assess the level of rigidity of the over-determined solution. In turn, this helps inform us how carefully we must frame interventions so as not to evoke underlying feelings of shame, self-punishment, or urges to retaliate.

Quadrant Two Is a Depiction of Patients' Failed Attempts to Distance From Feelings that Leave Them Frightened and Vulnerable

Quadrant Two identifies clusters of symptoms that break through into conscious (dystonic) awareness. As seen, the absolutes of Quadrant One inevitably clash with reality and lead to intensive disillusionment, corrosive self-hate, pain, shame, or panic. Symptoms can be understood as attempts to distance from the intensity of said feeling states by the use of addictive numbing mechanisms, over-work to the point of exhaustion, and depressive withdrawal. In other words, symptoms offer both a break from the pressures and demands contained in Quadrant One as well as throwing the pre-existing compulsively created homeostatic balance out of kilter.

Quadrant Two

Symptoms

DEPRESSIVE CLUSTER
Ranging from dysthymia to hopelessness and despair

BEHAVIORAL CLUSTER
Exhaustion, deprivation, lack of self-care

ANXIETY CLUSTER
Confusion, inertia, paralysis, fear of emptiness

SOMATIC CLUSTER
Addictions, body dysmorphia, eating disorders

Figure 4.3 Quadrant Two
*Reprinted with permission from the book *Listening with Purpose: Entry Points into Shame and Narcissistic Vulnerability*, (p. 43), J. Danielian & P. Gianotti, Lanham, Jason Aronson, 2012.

Although bio-based symptoms can be involved, both owned and disowned absolutes may certainly also be involved. As have been observed by many, the levels of self-loathing to which one can descend are very significantly related to the depth of how much one has experienced the absolutes as the *only* thing keeping hope alive and therefore making life itself possible.

Dynamic Assessment

There are a number of factors that help the therapist formulate an initial assessment as to the level of rigidity and fragility of the character organization as measured through Quadrant Two.

- Does the patient express his puzzlement over the dystonic breakthrough of symptoms through language that conveys almost a superhuman belief that no matter how he treats his body and psyche, he should be strong enough to withstand what others cannot endure? In other words, is there a hidden desire for invincibility?

- Does the patient have a strong wish for you to "fix" the symptoms *without* tampering with any of her own rigidly held behavioral or belief systems?
- Is there a heightened resistance to the suggestion of medication, even though there may be a significant family history within any given symptom cluster?
- Are behavioral or somatic patterns minimized with a sense of pride in being able to endure adversity? If the therapist tries to point out that these patterns may actually exacerbate the eruption of the symptom, does the patient express doubt or disbelief?
- Is there an absence of clear memory as to whether previous life strategies or circumstances resulted in the eruption of similar symptoms?

Video Case Vignette Illustrating Breakthrough of Quadrant Two

Please refer to the Routledge website, Video 4.2: Somaticizing.

In the following case vignette, we encounter a patient who presents with somatic complaints when work stressors continue to mount. The patient's inability to tolerate any decrease in his capacity to handle pressure is compounded by his reluctance to seek help. In his mind, both are tantamount to a sign of failure. When the therapist moves to inquire about feeling states, we see a severe somatic reaction being triggered. Ironically, his somatic reaction keeps him from developing a conscious awareness of his feelings more directly while simultaneously increasing his anxiety about physical concerns.

Patient: I don't even know why I'm here today. My doctor told me I had to come.

Therapist: Your doctor told you that you *had* to come?

Patient: Well, she didn't *force* me to come. She just said that there was nothing wrong with my heart, and that she thought my symptoms of chest pains and heart palpitations were caused by anxiety. I think that's a bunch of nonsense. I've never been an anxious person. I've always prided myself on my ability to handle pressure. At work I juggle a million balls in the air every day. I'm not anxious. I don't FEEL anxious. I've never been anxious.

Therapist: Has your situation at work changed recently?

Patient: What do you mean?

Therapist: Have you been given more responsibilities, or is there some deadline that may be pressuring you?

Patient: Well, now that you mention it, we are having a five-year review from corporate next month. My sales division hasn't been functioning up to their usual standard. Larry left last week, saying he

68

couldn't take the pressure any longer. What a loser. And here he leaves me in the lurch, that loser.

Therapist: You sound a little upset.

Patient: Darn right, I'm upset. I have a right to be upset. . . . Oh, my God. I can't catch my breath. It's happening again. It's like I can't get enough air.

Therapist: Why don't you slow down and try taking a couple of deep breaths. That's better.

Patient: See this is what happens when I start to talk about things that upset me. Do you think I have a weak heart? Do you think my doctor is wrong? Maybe I should go to another cardiologist.

Therapist: Has your doctor suggested medication for anxiety to see if your symptoms can be relieved?

Patient: I don't believe in taking that stuff. What, are you going to try to push pills on me too? I'm telling you I'm fine. I'm not anxious. I may be a little more stressed at work, but I've handled these kinds of situations before. I just need to ride it out.

Therapist: Do you think that if you talked about some of the stress in here, it might help you ride it out a little easier?

Patient: I don't know. Maybe. I guess I could use a neutral third party to hear me out. I can't really talk about these things at work. I'm the manager, and people look to me for answers.

Therapist: Do you have any friends you can talk to, your wife?

Patient: Oh, no. I would never burden her. Talk about anxiety. Now, there's a basket case. She cries when the least little thing goes wrong. No, I've got to be the strong one in the family. I take pride in it.

Therapist: You take pride in it, and yet you don't have anyone to talk to?

Patient: Yeah, that about sums it up. Maybe it would be a good idea to unload a little bit.

Questions for Analysis

1. How might you make further inquiries into the patient's statement, "My doctor told me I had to come?"

2. Discuss how tracking this statement is important in terms of:

   a. The patient's guardedness about therapy.

b. Future transferential dynamics.

c. The emergence of symptoms stemming from the patient's self-image as seen in Quadrant One.

3. How can you use the patient's statement about "unloading a bit" to help mitigate any feelings of shame around his self-image and reliance on others?

Summary of Quadrant Two

Although patients often enter into treatment through Quadrant Two and ask for symptom relief, many therapists have asked us whether patients actually derive some comfort from maintaining their symptoms. Certainly, symptoms cause distress, but it is often true that symptoms actually allow some patients to temporarily let go of their driven quest for perfection. It is as if the symptom allows them a break from inner pressure. However, the costs associated with this breakthrough are heavy. The therapeutic task is not only to help the patient deal with intrapsychic and interpersonal stress created from over-idealized expectations of self and others. It is also important to help the patient realize that the eruption of symptoms may be a symbolic *cry for help*, drawing attention to the fact that former over-determined efforts are exacting too great a cost to overall well-being.

The therapeutic tasks associated with Quadrant Two are summarized as follows:

- To help the patient learn (over time) that over-determined efforts toward perfectionistic standards actually can stem from feelings of underlying shame. These over-determined drives substantially contribute to symptom formation. But the reverse can occur as well, where the symptoms themselves function to provide a distraction from underlying fears of shameful inadequacy.

- To empathically assess, with the patient, ways in which he or she can replace self-destructive coping mechanisms with healthier lifestyle changes that attend to self-care.
- To help patients learn better strategies of affect-regulation. With individuals who have a trauma history, an additional delicate task is to help them learn strategies of ameliorating the intensity of symptoms. This can lead to improvements in self-esteem, a sense of internal stability, and progress around greater therapeutic integration over time.
- To help patients understand that symptoms often have important symbolic meaning. Once accepted, this leads to improving insight as well as accelerated integration between the quadrants. Eliminating symptoms, per se, often does not address issues of self-identity and self-cohesion. Unless patients understand the symbolic or dissociated communication from within the split-off parts of the self, integration and the emergence of the authentic self may be thwarted.

Quadrant Three

Loyal Waiting

- For the "perfect" idealized other

- For fantastical wishes for happiness or salvation

- For outside recognition of the purity of one's own self-sacrifice

- Wish for absolute answers, assurances, guarantees

- Rescue from pain & suffering

- A confusion between hidden, grandiose wishes and the real self

Figure 4.4 Quadrant Three
Reprinted with permission from the book *Listening with Purpose: Entry Points into Shame and Narcissistic Vulnerability*, (p. 47), J. Danielian & P. Gianotti, Lanham, Jason Aronson, 2012.

A more detailed discussion involving the fluidity between all of the quadrants and how they influence each other can be found at the end of this chapter.

Quadrant Three Is a Depiction of Loyal and Hopeful Waiting, Unexamined and Compulsively Held

Quadrant Three has been described as the quadrant that focuses on an individual's relational expectations of others and how he or she treats people in those relationships.

With narcissistic damage, the patient's inner beliefs and expectations of others represent a "relational pseudo-solution," where present-day relationships are meant to make up for failed relational attachments from the past. This *interpersonal* investment in a relational pseudo-solution is what creates habituated patterns that often lead to disappointment and frustration.

On the level of "wish-fulfillment," these pseudo-solutions may also involve the desire for salvation and rescue, hopefully achieved through finding the "perfect" idealized other. The increased conscious awareness of the pain that results from trying to meet grandiose expectations becomes more overt as the treatment progresses. Over time, the patient paradoxically experiences breakthroughs around having the courage to expose the idealized aspirations for self and other. As the therapy unfolds, relief partially comes from sharing these insights with the therapist.

As can be expected, Quadrant Three requires a long working-through process, as interpersonal issues of trust and loyalty become engaged. Again, we will provide carefully selected videotaped examples of the working-through process of Quadrant Three as the training proceeds.

Successful engagement in Quadrant Three becomes optimal when dimensions of the other quadrant sub-systems have begun to be processed and brought into conscious awareness. For example, an increase in a patient's self-reflective capacity around aspirations and goals, and their effect on symptoms and personal self-care, may be a prerequisite to allowing the therapist to move more directly into conversation about issues of loyalty and expectations of others. Often issues of loyalty, or loyally waiting for rescue from "the other," remain hidden from view until the patient feels safe enough in the therapeutic relationship to begin expressing longings or disappointments directly. Eventually, these longings become enacted within the therapeutic relationship.

Quadrant Three and the Therapeutic Relationship

Quadrant Three tends to be the "home" of transference. It is where important transferential enactments within the treatment relationship allow for longings and loyalty issues to emerge. The spontaneous forces of health that are inherent in the individual begin to take stronger foothold as the treatment progresses. This occurs even though greater dynamic depths of difficult and uncomfortable conflicts around early attachment patterns and loyalties are simultaneously being played out. This conflict between old loyalty patterns and new relational experiences gained within the safe holding environment of therapy coexist side-by-side for a period of time.

The therapist's role in monitoring micro-changes moment-to-moment is especially important, highlighting again the crucial role we have assigned to empathically attuned listening. Attuned listening in Quadrant Three frequently requires the therapist to anticipate disappointed expectations. These expectations are often hidden from the treatment early on but begin to emerge as the patient gains trust in the treatment alliance.

We can recognize early signs of hidden expectations and frustration through the patient's framework of "loyal waiting." Patients may begin to articulate that they are loyally waiting for rescue from others, but eventually, they will reveal the wish for rescue from the therapist as well.

As the therapist is able to give voice to this wish by asking generic questions about loyalty, the patient can allow for more hidden transferential longings to emerge in the treatment. Once the therapist wonders in subtle ways what will happen if the waiting for rescue bears no fruit, we may see signs of the eventual emergence of Quadrant Four.

As well, once loyal waiting begins to emerge more intensely in Quadrant Three, we may see both a resurgence of symptoms in Quadrant Two and a heightened investment in over-idealized self-aspirations from Quadrant One.

Video Case Vignettes Illustrating Quadrant Three

Here are two case illustrations that highlight the emergence of Quadrant Three in the evolving treatment. The first reveals the patient's loyal waiting as the therapist inquires about the "rules" contained within the old loyalty system versus those in a newly forming loyalty based on emerging authenticity. The second illustrates a patient who reverts to over-determined efforts in Quadrant One. Notice how the therapist handles this particular dynamic.

Please refer to the Routledge website, Video 4.3: Old Loyalties & Emerging Self—Part One.

Patient: I saw my mother while I was visiting Chicago this weekend.
Therapist: How did that go?
Patient: Well, it was typical. I don't know why I should be surprised.
Therapist: What do you mean typical?
Patient: So, I told her to meet me for lunch at this cute restaurant I knew about. I thought she would like the food, try something different for a change.

Therapist: Yes, and what happened?

Patient: I got there a little early, so I went inside to wait for her. She didn't show up on time, so I went to the window, and there she was waiting outside. I could tell she was irritated. So I went out and got her, and we got seated and all, and she said, "Why don't we order some appetizers?" So, I made a few suggestions. "How about we split some crab cakes?" "Nah, I don't like them." "Have you ever tried them?" "No, but I don't like them." "How do you know if you have never tried them?" "No, I don't want them." "How about shrimp dumplings?" "I don't like dumplings." "How about some raviolis? There's a nice looking spinach ravioli with cream sauce." "You know I hate spinach." I tell you, she is so limited. She's never willing to venture outside of her familiar box.

Therapist: So, you were a little frustrated? A little disappointed?

Patient: I don't know why I should be disappointed. She's never going to change. And then she asked me how I was doing. I decided to be honest with her about my work. I told her I wasn't sure that I wanted to continue practicing law. She looked at me blankly. Then I said, "I know that you and dad really were happy when I decided to go to law school." She said, "We never wanted you to go to law school. That was your friend Andrea who gave you that idea." Of course, it wasn't Andrea, but she makes it seem that every move I make has to do with me listening to Andrea. She hated Andrea.

Therapist: What do you think that was all about?

Patient: Hating Andrea? It was because I was listening to someone other than her.

Therapist: Did you think about challenging her on this reconstruction of history?

Patient: What do you mean?

Therapist: Well, I'm wondering what she might have said if you said, "Do you mean that you and Dad didn't take any pleasure in seeing your daughter become a lawyer?"

Patient: It wouldn't have done any good. She would have just gotten defensive.

Therapist: (Long pause) So, what happened next?

Patient: She asked me about my relationship with Stan. I told her we were working out some issues and put the wedding on hold. She then said, "You know, I just want you to be happy." And I said, "Well, we're working on things so we make sure we're making the right decision to move forward." Again she said, "I just want you to be happy." And she said, "You know, there's an old saying—'shit or get off the pot.' You're not getting any younger. Have you thought about children?" And I said, "Mom, I think I'm not ready. We've talked about it, and we're not going to try to have kids right now."

Then I said, "Mom, are you happy?" And she said, "I've never really been happy. I've had a miserable life." Then she said, "Well, I was happy when you were born. And I'd be happy if I had a grandchild." Then, I realized this whole concern about me being happy was really about *her*, her wanting a grandchild. That's the way it goes with us. It's all about her, but then, I think about her sitting there in the restaurant, and that's where I get confused. She looks so desperate, so needy to have contact with me. (Pause) I do think she loves me in her own pathetic way.

Therapist: You know, I just had this image of the two of you sitting in that restaurant. Here is this woman, your mother, and what I think you're trying to tell me through this interchange is that you're frustrated because she is really such a limited vessel. Maybe one way we can think about this is that she's trying to offer you a cup, a cup of holding because that's what mothers are supposed to do, hold you so you can feel support and grow and thrive. But, she is such a small vessel; she has such a small cup that is trying to hold this very big, talented, beautiful, bright daughter. She could never hold all that you are in such a small container.

Patient: (Begins to sob) (Long pause, and in a very soft voice) I think you're right. (Softly) I like that image. (Looks up and smiles)
Please refer to the Routledge website, Video 4.4: Old Loyalties & Emerging Self—Part Two.

Patient: I'd like to pick up where we left off last week. What you said was very moving (pause) and accurate.

Therapist: Moving. Moving in what way?

Patient: I always knew that something never felt right with my mother. I was constantly upset as a child that I didn't have a good relationship with my mother. I was worried that I would do something that she wouldn't approve of; then she'd get critical and she'd withdraw from all of us. Sometimes she wouldn't speak to us for days. I was always trying to be a good kid, study hard, but down deep I knew that I lacked the confidence in myself that other people had. I could see that other parents built their kids up. Andrea's mother, for instance, always built her up, was so accepting of her and of me too. I never understood why my mother was always so critical and controlling. (Looks up) But maybe she didn't know how to do anything differently. Maybe she was just too small of a container. (Pause) It makes it easier to understand. There's less blame and anger when I think of it that way.

Therapist: I hope you didn't hear what I said as you not having a right to be frustrated or angry. You still didn't get what you needed from her as a mother.

Patient: No, there's no point in getting angry. It's just a sad situation. It's just really sad.

Therapist: Yes, it is very sad, sad that you didn't get what you needed and sad that your mother has limited capacity to love unconditionally. But, one thing I'd like to focus on is that because of your mother's limited capacity, you learned that you had to adapt to your mother's need to keep you small in order to have any relationship at all.

Patient: (Long pause) Yes, yes. I think that's exactly right. That's why I keep getting frustrated with her over and over again. I keep hoping that she will grow like I have grown. It's useless. I give up.

Therapist: Useless? Give up? I'm not so sure any of us give up on these wishes so easily. Sometimes we just transfer that longing onto other relationships. Maybe we can begin to think about how this pattern might play out in other relationships in the present day.

Patient: What do you mean?

Therapist: Where you're made to feel small. As a little girl, you learned not to make waves or to ask for too much, to be a good girl. You said to me that as a child you were very shy. But I'm wondering if part of that shyness was really a fear to speak up because it wasn't very safe to do so.

Patient: No, I think that was just my basic temperament.

Therapist: I'm sure temperament does factor into the mix as well. But you know, I haven't experienced you as being all that shy in here.

Patient: Really? Do you think so?

Therapist: Well, have you found that it's been difficult speaking up in here?

Patient: No, I guess not, now that you mention it. But I do with other people. I mean, I feel that I play it safe at work, and I let the paralegals get away with not doing all of their work, and it gets dumped on me. And sometimes in my relationship with my fiancé, Stan, he makes me feel so confused . . . that I can't find the words to explain myself.

Therapist: You can't find the words to explain yourself, and you are calling this a matter of you being shy? Can you give me an example of how this happens?

Patient: Well, the other day, I asked him if he needed help with paying for our vacation, the one we're taking with his kids, and he said no, he was all set. He would pay for his daughters, that it wasn't my responsibility. Then two days later, he gets his American Express bill, and I can tell that he's worrying about money. He doesn't say anything, but he gets irritable over little things. I start to feel like I can't do anything right. He starts complaining about my car being such a mess, and I left underwear on the bathroom floor.

I didn't say anything, but then I had an opportunity to go back into the city to see my old roommate from Chicago. I asked Stan if he wanted to go, but he said no, he couldn't afford it. Then he said, "It must be nice for you to be on an attorney's salary and just be able to pick up and go whenever you feel like it." It made me feel a little guilty, but I know I shouldn't be feeling guilty. I had offered to help pay for our vacation. See, that's where I get confused.

Therapist: Did you point this discrepancy out to him?

Patient: No, not right away. These exchanges happen so quickly that I need time to think about it, to make sense out of it myself. Later, I tried to talk about it, I brought it back up, and he accused me of holding onto things, internalizing, that I let things stew, or he says that I'm being too sensitive. Then, I feel guilty for not being able to speak up in the moment.

Therapist: But you didn't feel any anger toward his unfairness?

Patient: No, not really. I just let it pass.

Therapist: Do you see how this pattern is a little bit like what you learned to do with your mother?

Patient: (Long pause) Yes, I guess I do. I wouldn't have put the two things together, but I do feel a similar shut-down feeling.

Therapist: That's what I meant earlier when I said the more important thing is to pay attention to how this trigger of being forced into a smaller container might play itself out in the present.

Questions for Discussion

Session One

1. Identify signs of the patient's longings toward her mother in the context of her mother's behavior at the luncheon.

2. In general, how is her expression of frustration actually evidence of loyalty issues as described in Quadrant Three?

3. *Discuss how early signs of breaking the loyalty dilemma begin to surface when the patient asks her mother if she is happy?*

4. *Describe how the patient's statement, "Well, I guess she loves me in her own pathetic way," puts her back into a state of "loyal waiting."*

5. *How does the therapist's comment about the mom being a limited vessel, not being able to hold all of who the daughter is, help the patient loosen the grip of the loyalty bond?*

Second Session

1. *In the second session, what are the possible risks if the patient moves away from her frustration or anger too quickly? (Notice how this pattern continues to play itself out at work and in her relationship.)*

2. *How does the wish to help her mother grow continue the old loyalty dilemma?*

3. *Notice how the patient continues to revert to "temperamental shyness" as a way of maintaining an old homeostatic balance. What effect do you think that the therapist's comment of not experiencing the patient as "shy" has on the old loyalty bind?*

Analysis

In this two-session case vignette we see how the back and forth between new insight and old loyalty bonds weave in and out of the dialogue. The discovery and assertion of the authentic self is often tentative at first. This is fairly typical in working with Quadrant Three relational dynamics.

The human need to preserve connection is strong, and individuals with insecure attachments experience the exquisite struggle between maintaining connection at all cost and being validated for one's authentic self. As conflict ensues, loyalty dilemmas emerge and are re-enacted in present-day relationships.

When individuals enter therapy due to current relationship struggles, loyalty patterns around what is permissible and what threatens to fracture connection can begin to emerge quite early. In this case example, the therapist's challenge is to work with the patient's frustration and disappointment in a way that does not overwhelm the patient in the moment. Using the metaphor of "limited vessel" helps the patient differentiate without retaliating in frustration against the mother.

Instead, it allows the patient's feelings of sadness to begin to emerge, which in turn creates an opening for the patient to make movements toward differentiation without the fear of cutting ties with her mother completely. However the therapist anticipates the potential risk of the patient sweeping negative feelings under the rug. She works to maintain a stance of curiosity with the patient by helping her see the connection between her relationship with her mother and a similar pattern that plays out at work and in her primary relationship.

Summary of Quadrant Three

Quadrant Three represents aspects of the psyche that depict relational dynamics from the vantage point of the character solution. Thus, "loyal waiting" captures the longing for a relationship that will either repair past damage or live up to perfect, idealized standards. Both of these over-determined positions are attempts at preventing the experience of disappointment or pain around relational connection.

Loyal waiting may also reflect a deep-seated wish for rescue. At times this wish may be quite overt, or the patient's longing may be masked by a learned response of caretaking and serving others at the expense of self. The patient's hope in this scenario is that if enough caretaking is given, the "other" will eventually provide love and nurturance in return.

Yet another variant of the longing associated with Quadrant Three may manifest as entitled, impatient demands for the "other" to meet the person's needs *as if by magic*. In this presentational style, the individual often has difficulty asking for needs to be met directly, as the need to ask is in itself experienced as shameful.

Because of these varying styles of loyal waiting, the therapist may become confused by or miss one of the manifestations of loyal waiting. We have found that reviewing a series of questions related to Quadrant Three dynamics can help ameliorate some of this confusion. Thus, the therapeutic tasks associated with Quadrant Three are summarized as follows:

- Is the patient able to see others in a reality-based context, or is the "other" overly idealized or overly distrusted?
- Does the patient reflexively assume blame or personal responsibility for another person's shortcomings, mistreatment, or mistakes?
- Does the patient believe that he or she can "fix" the other person?
- Does the patient compulsively detach from others and demonstrate a belief that avoidance is a positive strategy?
- Are the patient's expectations of others realistic and reasonable?

Quadrant Four

Revenge Enactments

- ◆ Grossly self-damaging behaviors ranging from neglect to suicidal acts

- ◆ Wish to harm others, ranging from devaluation to acts of violence

- ◆ Sabotage of success (self or other)

- ◆ Repeated testing/demands of proof

- ◆ Self-hate due to disillusionment or humiliation

- ◆ Externalization of blame

Figure 4.5 Quadrant Four
Reprinted with permission from the book *Listening with Purpose: Entry Points into Shame and Narcissistic Vulnerability*, (p. 49), J. Danielian & P. Gianotti, Lanham, Jason Aronson, 2012.

- When disappointed, how extreme is the patient's reaction? Are there signs that the patient has a desire to retaliate in order to "even the score"?
- Does the patient aspire to a capacity for mutuality and fairness in relationship?

Quadrant Four Is a Depiction of the Hidden Wish to Retaliate (Against Self or Others) When Confronted with Failed Attempts to Achieve Over-Idealized Expectations

Quadrant Four is often the most hidden of all of the quadrants. It can be either hidden from view of the therapist by design, or it can be hidden from the self in the form of dissociated and unintegrated material. The therapist can see early signs of Quadrant Four emerging by attending to the following:

- Does the patient continually compare himself or herself to others, where one or the other must come up short?
- Does the patient use a devaluing tone or become impatient very quickly?
- Does the patient set realistic limits and goals around self-care, or is there a driven standard imposed that is punishing or exhausting?
- Does the patient justify hurting others, or getting even with others, when disappointed?
- Does the patient justify aloneness and resignation?
- Is the idea of confrontation with "the other" scary or overly denied?

Quadrant Four is generally experienced as dystonic or foreign; therefore, it is often uncomfortable or less than consciously held. As such, patients reveal the "taboo" material only when feeling safe enough to trust that they will not be shamed or judged by the therapist. Careful exposure of the patient's secret longing for revenge, retaliation, or sabotage is an important and critical step in mitigating underlying feelings of shame.

Since these are all part of an idealized solution, the patient can experience mortifying shame and self-destructive impulses when unsavory aspects of retaliatory motives become exposed. Revealing Quadrant Four material holds the potential of threatening the therapeutic alliance, as the patient may fear being judged as a result of harboring "negative" wishes.

Increased conscious awareness of Quadrant Four also tests the former homeostatic loyalty balance found in Quadrant Three. In early childhood relationships, where unfairness or lack of safety was present, for many children the outward expression of anger or protest was never allowed. As the treatment progresses and secrets are faced, this outward manifestation of Quadrant Four actually reveals signs of emerging health and authenticity.

However, the therapist can be sorely tested at this juncture, as patients attempt to regain a sense of control by "going on the attack." For example, patients often make repeated demands for ironclad evidence of "proof" or challenge the therapist's credentials as a way of leveling the playing field of the relationship. The patient is ready to dismiss or discard previous gains, finding it difficult to hold in memory evidence of improving mood, increasing sense of authenticity, and recalling the safety and trust in the non-hierarchical therapeutic relationship.

The hard-won gains that stemmed from increasing insight and gradually integrating sub-systems often seem to be temporarily lost. It is important for the therapist not to lose hope that the treatment is helping. Actually, at later stages of the therapy, this is often evidence of a therapeutic breakthrough, something that must be played out in the treatment in order for the intensity of affect to become metabolized and neutralized.

We remember that such transferential mistrust reflects the patient's fears of traumatic exposure of dystonic impulses, beliefs, and idealizing mechanisms. The loss of ideals of perfection actively confronts the false illusions that parents imposed on the developing self of the child. In the long run, all of this is in the service of further integration, with the exposure of Quadrant Four being the most direct challenge to positive self-worth. It is where the impulses to punish or retaliate are often filled with feelings of shame and virulent self-hate. Working through the transferential enactments of Quadrant Four is where growth and integration are most palpable and enduring.

The therapeutic tasks associated with Quadrant Four are as follows:

- When Quadrant Four dynamics emerge in full force, the question for the therapist becomes how to steady oneself and the patient simultaneously. A useful question for the therapist to keep in mind is, "How can I not get triggered by my own feelings in the present moment?"
- A clinical question that the therapist can articulate to the patient is, "Can we remain patient and keep hope alive while these painful issues around abandonment and rejection (from childhood on) come to the surface?"
- The therapist's task is to maintain a deeply attuned immersion in the patient's pain without succumbing to therapeutic self-doubt, therapeutic despair, or therapeutic closure. (The question of therapeutic self-doubt is one that will be addressed over and over throughout the examples covered in this Workbook).
- This type of reaction is often confusing to therapists who have experienced a solid therapeutic alliance up to the point of the emergence of Quadrant Four. It is as if the memory of this deeply held and worked-for alliance is somehow forgotten by the patient. Yet, the patient *has to disconnect* in order to more fully experience a new and different environment in the treatment, a non-retaliatory one to support the patient's efforts to "wake" from a dissociative reenactment.

- The intersubjective dynamic between the therapist and the patient can lead to new neurotransmitter pathways in the present moment. Recent research has shown that this is achieved in psychotherapy through the systemic working-through of enactments.
- As has been mentioned, engagement in Quadrant Four can become a precarious point in many treatments. Yet, if handled successfully, it is often a major breakthrough that leads to further integration of dissociative splits and further claiming of the authentic self.
- This precarious juncture can be less threatening to the therapist if the therapist recalls the intimate connections between the other three quadrants leading up to this point. These connections can form a psychological holding pattern as the patient begins to react or retreat to Quadrant Four.

Video Case Vignettes Illustrating Quadrant Four

The next two video segments illustrate different manifestations of how Quadrant Four material might emerge within the treatment. The first case vignette provides an example of how Quadrant Four behaviors often blend with signs of emerging authenticity. In addition, this first video illustrates the rapid shifting between competitive behaviors turning outward, followed by an immediate shift to self-criticism, self-blame, and attempts to shrink the expression of the real self emerging. The second video reveals a more intentional wish to get even in order to "right the score." Although this behavior is aimed against the disappointing other, we also can view this as a breakthrough of emerging authenticity, as the patient is able to consciously disclose this desire to the therapist. Thus, what had been kept hidden from view is able to be processed relationally.

Please refer to the Routledge Website, Video 4.5: Someone Has to Be Sacrificed.

Background Information

The patient is a 45-year-old woman who has been in therapy for seven years. She entered therapy due to depression and difficulties in her marriage. During the course of treatment, the patient was able to end the marriage and successfully raise three children on her own. Although her own ambitions were sacrificed during this period, with the empty nest, she has been struggling with self-emergence around career and a new relationship.

By way of background, the patient was raised in an upper-middle-class family where appearance was everything, and there was a great deal of pressure to succeed. Her father died when the patient was in her early teens. When her father was alive, the patient remembers being his favorite, and she believed that her mother was jealous of their relationship.

Although her mother had always been critical and withholding of affection throughout the patient's childhood, when her father died, her mother became increasingly critical of her daughters and began to lean heavily on her only son, whom she idealized and granted special favors.

As children, the patient remembers that she and her two sisters tried to compete for her mother's attention, and she reports that her older sister "always won." "Winning" included competing with the patient, fabricating stories to get her into trouble, stealing boyfriends, and becoming mother's little helper. In high school after her father died, her mother began to exhibit increasingly intense outbursts that were often directed at her three daughters. It was at this point that the patient began to challenge her mother's inconsistencies and unfairness, in part trying to protect her sisters, which only made her a further target of her mother's contempt and criticism.

These particular details of the patient's history are included as they help set the stage for the following case vignette, which is an example of the patient/therapist dialogue around the conscious processing and integration of Quadrant Four dynamics.

Patient:	I'm still feeling tired, sad, and very down on myself. I know what you said last time, that this may be a reaction to taking a risk and letting people see more of my vulnerability, exposing more of who I am through my writing.
Therapist:	That was such a powerful piece of writing that you read to me last week.
Patient:	I know, I know. You're supposed to say stuff like that. But, I didn't get the response I was looking for. People praised me for my writing style, but they didn't say anything about *me*. Why would this devastate me so much? It's like I can't move. All I've been doing is crying.
Therapist:	What were you hoping people would say to you? (Pause) What were you hoping they would notice?
Patient:	I don't know. Maybe I wanted this one effort to make up for all of the times I was never noticed by my family. But that's a dead-end street, isn't it? No amount of praise or noticing will ever make up for that.
Therapist:	I think you're onto something here. Is that possibly what all the grief is about?
Patient:	I think that's part of it.
Therapist:	And?
Patient:	I'm afraid I'm too much for people. I'm afraid that whenever I do finally show more of what's really inside of me, people become intimidated. I'm afraid that when I finally do come out, I'll be too

much for people. They'll distance themselves from me because I'm too intense.

Therapist: Too intense? In what way?

Patient: Maybe it's that my needs are too intense; my desire to be noticed is too much. I'm afraid I'll just want to take up all of the air space and not give other people a chance to have their day in the sun. I'm afraid that if the focus shifts to someone else, I'll try to direct it back to myself, maybe by trying to make the most astute comment. (Pause) Or making a subtle criticism.

Therapist: Did something like that actually happen?

Patient: Well, not at the poetry reading, but last weekend I went out with my friends, Rhonda and Pauline. You know how Rhonda keeps encouraging me to mend fences with Pauline. But I don't trust Pauline after what she did to me last year. But I went anyway to please Rhonda. I was nervous because I know that Pauline gets very competitive with me. So, we were talking about politics, and I really did have a lot to say. I was pretty animated, and I felt that I showed more of myself. I thought the evening went ok. Then Rhonda called me very upset saying that I cut her off, and I diminished or ridiculed her whenever she voiced an opinion. When I thought about it, I realized that she was right. I felt horrible about myself. That's the part of me that is filled with disgust.

Therapist: You feel disgust about yourself?

Patient: Yes, yes. It's disgusting. It's that part of myself that's like Gollum in *The Lord of the Rings*, saying "My precious, my precious," but all the while my claws are out, and someone needs to be sacrificed.

Therapist: I'm confused. Why does someone always need to be sacrificed? Are you referring to all situations where you're with a group of people?

Patient: No, it never seems to happen with men. Only women.

Therapist: All women?

Patient: No, not all women. Just women who have a devious side to them. Women I don't trust.

Therapist: You mean like Pauline?

Patient: Yes. But, I didn't go after Pauline; I went after Rhonda. Why would I go after the weak ones?

Therapist: Were you a little afraid to challenge Pauline? I know that when you tried to talk to her last year, things didn't go so well.

Patient: That's part of it. I was nervous about seeing her. Maybe that's why I talked so much, like I needed to prove something to her, prove how smart I am.

Therapist: I know we've talked about Pauline reminding you of your mother.

Patient: Yes, but I took my mother on. I was the only one that challenged her directly.

Therapist: And she never accepted it. I mean, it did nothing to modify her behavior, to listen to you, to apologize, or to change. And also, when you were younger, you did try to get her to notice you, to see how smart you were, to see you for you.

Patient: You're right. But, that doesn't explain why I went after Rhonda. See, I'm disgusting. I hate this part of myself. It's like I can't receive anything, including acknowledging that I'm big, that I'm intelligent. It's me, I know it's the real me coming out, but it gets confused with the part of me that will do this at other people's expense. It's like those two parts of myself exist really close together inside of myself.

Therapist: Yes, I can see how it must feel that way to you. But, I also want to remind you, that when you were a teenager, when you tried to speak up, when you tried to challenge your mother's unfairness, none of your other siblings came to your defense.

Patient: No, you're right. They ran and hid. My younger sister told me years later that they all knew I was trying to protect them.

Therapist: But nobody came to your defense.

Patient: No, nobody did. (Realization) Just like Rhonda . . . she didn't come to my defense either. Last year, when Pauline went ballistic at that party, yelling at me, drunk as a skunk, Rhonda did nothing. Then later, she tried to minimize Pauline's behavior, saying it was just the alcohol talking. She keeps trying to pretend that nothing happened. That I'm supposed to pretend that nothing happened. Just like in my family. They're still all pretending. We're supposed to get together at holidays and reunions and be one big happy family. Everyone ignores mom's jabs.

Therapist: So, maybe you're telling me that you also have some resentment for Rhonda not coming to your defense, for your siblings not coming to your defense. Are you worried that if you don't sacrifice someone in a potentially unsafe situation, you will become the one that is sacrificed?

Patient: Yeah, yeah. I always believe there has to be a sacrifice. I was the living sacrifice in my family, wasn't I?

Questions for Review

1. *Discuss why the patient might be feeling tired and sad after a successful reading of her poetry the week before.*

a. How might this be a way to regulate feelings of shame for wanting more from people?

b. Do you see how this may be a tamping down of the real self—a reflex reaction around breaking the old loyalty contract of "self-sacrifice" in Quadrant Three?

c. How might this also be a way of taking her desires to be seen and turning against herself by labeling her need as "disgusting"?

2. Explain how feelings of hopelessness may emerge around the patient's struggle to be seen and validated.

3. Highlight ways that the therapist tracks and connects the various parts of the patient's history to her behavior with Rhonda and Pauline.

4. How does the therapist help to modulate the patient's feelings of shame around the Quadrant Four behavior of the patient's comment—"Someone always needs to be sacrificed"?

The next case example offers an illustration of a direct breakthrough of Quadrant Four. It should be emphasized that the direct verbal emergence of Quadrant Four within the treatment is actually a sign of progress. Whenever a patient makes a verbal admission of "taboo" or shameful material, this admission is evidence of growing trust in the strength of the therapeutic bond. In addition, it is a sign that material once kept hidden from view can be brought into the light of day. More will be said on this issue of health within non-health in our chapter on transference.

Please refer to the Routledge website, Video 4.6: Getting Even.

Background Information

In this case vignette the patient has been in therapy twice a week for several years. Throughout the course of treatment the patient tested boundaries with women, often younger or unavailable women, only to be disappointed time and again. This patient also exhibited a pattern of becoming overly involved in relationships at work, where he would over-commit and spend long hours on projects, hoping to be noticed or praised for his "efforts beyond the call of duty." When praise was not forthcoming or he felt that he wasn't validated enough, the patient would often withdraw in anger, either retaliating verbally or distancing from the relationship completely.

In terms of the therapeutic interaction, the patient often "tested" the relationship by asking for additional time beyond his session limit, asking questions and then becoming angry if the therapist answered his question directly or conversely if she asked him for further clarification. Furthermore, any conscious experience of dependency or neediness quickly invoked feelings of shame followed by a struggle, the patient trying to get the therapist to apologize or admit that she could have said something in a better way. Eventually, the patient was able to consciously hold his feelings of neediness more directly, and he was able to confess that reliance on others made him feel small, babyish, or pathetic.

Over the course of repeated encounters of testing the therapeutic alliance, expressing disappointment or devaluing the therapist's abilities, the steadiness of the therapist's neutral, non-retaliatory stance allowed the patient to reveal more material from Quadrant Three and Quadrant Four directly. In addition, the patient was able to tolerate feelings of shame around his neediness with less self-deprecation. However, his pushing the boundaries with women continued. Although the therapist continued to mirror this pattern back to the patient, he seemed to hold onto his "right to do it my way" posture. In this session, the therapist is challenging the patient's choices more directly. As a result, a more direct breakthrough of Quadrant Four emerges.

Discussion Questions

1. How do you understand the patient's pattern of testing relationships through his repeated, unrealistic demands? Specifically, discuss how this

---

> *pattern reflects both a manifestation of unrequited wishes in Quadrant Three and a manifestation of retaliation in Quadrant Four?*
>
> *2. How does the repeated use of this pattern of testing people function as an attempt to keep feelings of shame and neediness under the surface?*
>
> *3. How might you try to penetrate the patient's posture of doing it his way?*
>
> *4. What might be an appropriate follow-up remark to the patient's admission of deriving satisfaction in "making people suffer"?*

Analysis

Evening the score in life, as an attempt to avoid direct exposure to feelings of shame, is a circular, repeating pattern. Unless and until the wish for revenge is consciously owned and articulated directly in treatment, Quadrant Four cannot be metabolized. This metabolism process occurs through revealing a "taboo" shameful wish in hopes that the therapist will not "retaliate" by passing negative judgment, thus inducing further shaming.

This vignette is an example of a breakthrough in the treatment. Once the wish to make another suffer was revealed and processed without humiliation, the patient was able to let go of his defiant position of doing it his way. In addition this admission freed the patient to explore more directly his longings in Quadrant Three. He did this by exploring connections to early parental failures around their lack of availability and their preoccupation with their own anxiety. Thus, he realized that his parents' wish for their son to become the savior and success story of the family was an attempt to compensate for their own feelings of inadequacy. This in turn allowed the patient to let go of self-imposed pressures in Quadrant One, setting more realistic goals for himself, which in turn obviated further shameful disappointments when the patient wasn't praised to his satisfaction.

SUPERVISION VIDEOS ILLUSTRATING THE UTILITY OF THE FOUR QUADRANT MODEL

In these final vignette examples in Chapter 4, we offer two examples of supervisory dialogue to help readers further integrate the application of the model into their practice.

The first video is a segment of a group supervision session illustrating how the Four Quadrant Model can be applied to short-term cognitive-behavioral orientations. The second video acts as an integrative summary wrap-up to our discussion of the Four Quadrant Model. In the second video, the authors and the supervisee discuss the inter-relationship between the quadrants. The supervisee is able to articulate how *seeing the big picture* helps the patient feel more securely held by the therapeutic process.

Please refer to the Routledge website, Video 4.7: Consultation Session on Four Quadrant Model and Short-Term Therapy.

ANALYSIS

In this video of a group supervision session, we see a supervisee who was initially trained in short-term cognitive-behavioral therapy. After six months of group supervision on how to apply the Four Quadrant Model to short-term therapy, we see how this therapist's listening attention and his conceptualization of the treatment begin to subtly change. Notice how Jack's question around directing him back to connecting parental messages with the therapist's observations around loyalty in the present moment begins to link the past to the present. Notice also Patricia's observations as to how quickly the supervisee has begun to organically move around the quadrants.

In our experience, therapists who were initially trained in non-psychodynamic models are surprisingly quick to adapt the Four Quadrant Model into their orientation and approach with patients. Even in a brief period of time, when tuned into the interplay of the quadrants, therapists are able to see the interconnection between the quadrants as well as be alert to what is missing from the picture. They frequently report that this is helpful in terms of knowing where to dig or knowing what questions to ask, in order that a fuller picture of the patient's psyche can be revealed.

Even in brief therapy, as was true with this case example, we can see how quickly Quadrant Three and Four were activated and became a part of the dialogue in the present moment. Pay attention to how Patricia points this dynamic out when she focuses in on the patient's reaction of disappointment. By

90

attending to the patient's language around disappointment, we observe how devaluing elements of Quadrant Four leak out when the patient describes his meeting with a friend as "worthless."

When applying the Four Quadrant Model to short-term therapy, issues of timing, the pace of therapy, and how far to dig into the excavation process must be monitored very carefully. This is especially true when issues of self-destructiveness or lability of affect are at play. Nevertheless, the Four Quadrant Model is useful as a diagnostic tool as well as providing an expanded roadmap into seeing more aspects of the psyche.

Please refer to the Routledge website, Video 4.8: Consultation Summary on Systemic Wrap-up of Four Quadrant Model.

Discussion Questions

1. *What do you think the supervisee means by the Four Quadrant Model providing a way of staying closer to where the patient is in the present moment?*

2. *How does the model provide checks and balances—a way of not getting lost in the details?*

3. *How can seeing the holistic picture act as a "check-point" if the therapist feels stuck in the treatment?*

4. *From the perspective of tracking psychological dynamics, what does Jack mean when he states that the Four Quadrant Model is a "process grid"?*

5. *How might the Four Quadrant Model provide a way to help you see what you might be missing in the treatment?*

SUMMARY: THE INTERCONNECTIVITY OF THE FOUR QUADRANT MODEL IN ACTION

The need for a Four Quadrant Model of psychotherapy became clear to us when we reviewed various handbooks of psychotherapy, both past and present. The struggle to incorporate the experiential realities critical to the practice of psychotherapy is an ongoing battle. We began to realize that at every moment in the treatment process, multiple forces are vitally operating, each at times pressing for recognition. The relationship between forces is inherently circular and systemic. All are parts of a whole. It goes without saying that all are critical to the outcome of treatment.

What are these forces? Traditionally we have been told that the goal of therapy is to make unconscious forces conscious. But not all conscious forces are healthy, as demonstrated in Quadrant One.

Drives for idealized perfection, syntonic absolutes, and rigid belief systems in Quadrant One can all be consciously experienced and valorized as utterly praise-worthy. Of course, the dystonic forces of Quadrant Two (hopelessness, despair, exhaustion, confusion) are also mainly conscious forces that the patient wants desperately to eliminate. These painful conflicts, potentially life-threatening, can best be addressed in the intersubjective moment-to-moment experience of the patient.

For example, as has been noted, Quadrant One and Quadrant Two describe sub-systems comprising a larger system that has not yet become consciously connected with Quadrant Three and Quadrant Four. Although all of the Quadrants are connected to shame, in the early phase of treatment, Quadrants Three and Four remain under the surface of conscious awareness for the most part. As the therapy progresses, the interconnectivity between Quadrant Three and Quadrant Four begins to take hold. That is, the intrapsychic system gradually begins to *incorporate* (not replace) the relational interpersonal system.

Here is where loyalty issues become more strongly activated and enacted within the therapy itself. Armed with the newfound de-idealizing dimensions of Quadrant Four, the patient engages the therapist more directly in the relational working through of the character pathology in Quadrant Three. This direct engagement within the relationship gives the therapist an opportunity to work through dissociated or disconnected aspects of the psyche toward further integration and a more secure relational attachment system.

From a systemic viewpoint, the relationship between any of the quadrants is not linear, despite being numerically identified. As we noted earlier, the relationships of the quadrants are circular, fluid, and systemic, with multiple feedback loops. For example, there is no actual linear movement between Quadrant One and Quadrant Two. Rather, as treatment evolves, a systemic understanding would encompass Quadrant One "absorbing" Quadrant Two into a larger system. That is, the patient grows to tolerate symptoms to a greater degree because the symptoms have become less dissociated.

Similarly, as treatment further continues, the larger system becomes even more expanded with the absorption of Quadrant Three, the quadrant that describes the therapeutic and dynamic *interpersonalizing* of character pathology, and eventually Quadrant Four, the quadrant with major de-idealizing angst. It is at this point that important relational issues such as loyalty and the therapeutic alliance, transference (positive, negative, or both), and counter-transference are systemically engaged and become critical to the healing process.

If movements are systemic, could a patient coming into treatment be heavily invested in Quadrant One, heavily disinvested or in denial in Quadrant Two, and move rapidly into Quadrant Three or Quadrant Four? Indeed, yes, and these then become prognostic indicators of the level and type of character pathology.

Patients disavowing certain quadrants altogether are often more seriously entrenched in their character pathology and therefore more likely to resort to higher degrees of dissociation, denial, or disconnection.

As we tackle conflicts that emerge within the treatment, multiple forces come into play: the level of dissociation, the level of debilitating self-hating shame, and the often nascent forces of the authentic resilient self. These multiple forces reveal the Four Quadrant Model in action:

- **Dissociation can take many different forms, from micro-ruptures to more profound lapses in conscious awareness.** Without doubt, conscious awareness is an ambient state. As an example, the psychological profile may be that *cognitive* aspects of events are available but that the *emotional* components are dissociated. This is the case with many patients in treatment. On the other hand, traumatized patients frequently exhibit a profile where *cognitive* reconstruction of events is dissociated, but then seemingly disconnected *emotional* forces flood the patient. As well, we can note that dissociation and disavowal can come and go depending on the context, sometimes within the same session.

- **Self-hate and shame are at the epicenter of the Four Quadrant Model.** Initially fueled by conflicts both *within* Quadrant One and Quadrant Two and *between* these two quadrants, shame is often hidden by over-determined efforts to avoid the painful feeling altogether. Yet, as we can see from the case illustrations provided, disavowed shame fuels the protective defenses of narcissistic overcompensation and its resulting self-hate. An important impetus in treating individuals with narcissistic injury is to empathically access feelings of shame and self-hate as they emerge in the treatment process. Unexamined shame, as we now know, will continue to paralyze any constructive movement within quadrants and certainly *between* any of the four quadrants.

- Finally, the nascent forces of emerging real self are always present in any encounter and are in conflict with every aspect of the false-self construction. All of these healthy and unhealthy forces are creating intricate and iterating homeostatic balance points in treatment as the individual gradually gains confidence with the emerging authenticity. Needless to say, each increase in authenticity itself can create a punishing backlash of regressive forces trying to reestablish their former prominence.

Without adequate understanding of how all these forces are intricately involved in every time frame in therapy, any intervention becomes problematic. Yet once a person is in treatment, there is real cause for optimism. All the forces we have described are in conflict with each other on a *continuing* basis. Each conflict shows itself in every therapeutic encounter. Our present posture in the here-and-now offers us a *repeated* intimate glimpse of the moment-to-moment movement. With more intensive listening, we might say that the practice of psychotherapy itself teaches us how to do therapy.

In the next chapter we will focus on intensive training geared specifically to the deepening of therapeutic listening for each sub-system.

5

Three Techniques to Refine Therapeutic Listening and Tracking

When all is said and done, any psychotherapeutic approach is only as good as the therapist applying it. . . . It requires sensitivity to nuances that cannot be completely spelled out and a readiness to acknowledge that, whatever one's theoretical orientation, it is but a very provisional map of a vast and still largely unexplored territory.

—Wachtel (1993, p. 292)

Most therapists rely on a particular theoretical orientation as a foundation stone for their work. Chapter 5 introduces several intervention techniques that can be applied across therapeutic orientations to help deepen one's therapeutic listening skills. Whether your approach is cognitive-behavioral, dynamic, relational, or trauma-based, each technique identified in this chapter is aimed at increasing the clinician's capacity for greater *attunement* with the patient. Although we use the word *technique*, note that the techniques we recommend are intended to bring the therapist closer to an experience-near position. The greater the attunement in the present moment, the greater leverage one has for therapeutic change. Regardless of your treatment approach, deepening the therapeutic alliance is a strategy all therapies have in common.

THREE TECHNIQUES TO DEEPEN SKILLS IN LISTENING, TRACKING, AND INTERVENING

The following section will illustrate three techniques that will help sharpen your therapeutic listening skills, the tracking of dialogue, and the timing of interventions. It should be noted that these techniques are in line with Schore and Schore's (2012) approach addressing *right-brain-to-right-brain* communication. Furthermore, each technique described allows for greater impact around uncovering issues of shame sensitivity and narcissistic injury. A brief description of each technique is highlighted below. Each technique will subsequently be covered in greater detail. This will be followed-up with case vignettes to clarify and illustrate each intervention.

- **Entry Points**. This is *listening for key words* or phrases to help uncover hidden material or gain further clarification as to the patient's beliefs, assumptions, values, or defenses.
- **Moment-to-Moment Tracking**. This is *tracking the flow of dialogue* where the therapist looks for inconsistencies, contradictions, or movement away from material too quickly.
- **Forecasting**. This *is a "seeding operation."* It is a method where the therapist introduces a question or idea that is subliminally *aimed at penetrating habituated defensive patterns*. This can be helpful before patients are altogether ready to make a shift in their organizing schemas.

ENTRY POINTS

An entry point is a therapeutic opportunity to delve into the patient's use of language as a way of gaining further details of a patient's narrative. Gaining a deeper understanding of the nuances of the patient's communication is at the heart of therapeutic listening. In order to go deeper into the inquiry process, the therapist follows the conversation by tracking moment-to-moment shifts in the dialogue.

But what is it that we are tracking? Tracking involves listening for words or phrases that may reveal "the tip of an iceberg," so to speak. We may intuitively get the sense that something more is there, but it is communicated in a way that is often unclear, overgeneralized, or assumed.

The definition of an entry point is a way to use language as a tracking process to learn more about:

- How patients *think* and *organize* information.
- What they *perceive* and what they *fail to perceive*.
- The *affective* meaning of a given event.
- The *intensity* of frustrations and disappointments.
- The *speed* of their reactivity to a situation.
- Their *underlying assumptions* and *hidden expectations* of self and others.
- How the *idealized self-system* is organized.

When some aspect of the therapeutic communication doesn't make sense to us, or if the patient rapidly shifts from one point to the next, making it difficult to grasp the underlying meaning, or if the patient's tone changes abruptly, or if the patient suddenly seems to drift off, chances are we have discovered an entry point opportunity for deeper inquiry.

This is the time to *slow the process down*. Early on in our attempts to master this technique, therapists may or may not know if a word or phrase is an entry point. The entry point listening process involves waiting until the patient says something that isn't connecting for us. For example, this may involve the therapist pausing at such places in the dialogic exchange where a patient seems to have contradicted an earlier statement, or pausing to ask for further elaboration when something is not clear. When there is this lack of clarity, intuitively, we can tell ourselves that further attention is in order. By slowing the process down, our empathic inquiry continues the "entry-point process" of going deeper into hidden material allowing for more of the patient's thoughts and feelings to be revealed within the relational container of the therapeutic holding environment.

In many ways, slowing the process down is a natural outcome of therapy. As psychotherapy evolves, it characteristically slows *itself* down. Evolving therapy works with us! We point this out as encouragement to therapists that this process technique, after some experience, will feel natural in treatment and will gain its own momentum.

It is important to remember that patients have developed habituated mechanisms of overcompensation to keep split-off parts of the personality outside of their own conscious awareness and away from the negative scrutiny of others. As therapists, we try to find ways to create leverage to dismantle these tightly held mechanisms in the interest of patients' growth.

Split-off parts of the personality fuel narcissistic defenses. When the sense of self-inadequacy becomes too intense, it inevitably activates and triggers shame, either visible or hidden. Once necessary for self-stabilization and affect-regulation in childhood, the costs of narcissistic defenses in adulthood are great. This defense structure hinders the emergence of the authentic self and thereby hinders the process of integration and ongoing adult development.

The use of language as an "entry point" is intended to better penetrate dissociative processes in the service of integrating split-off material. Language as an entry point initially reveals *how* the "idealized self-system" is maintained. Until and unless the idealized self-system becomes more transparent in the therapeutic dialogue, it cannot be *metabolized, modified, or outgrown*.

The relinquishment or dismantling of elements of the "idealized self-system" is what makes way for the emergence of the authentic self. In this dismantling process, the patient and therapist together bring an increased curiosity to habituated patterns and assumptions, certainly including the difficulty in establishing the viability of one's own self-identity.

The use of language as an entry point into deeper dialogue is one window into the micro-level of our patients' subjective experience of the given moment.

HOW TO RECOGNIZE WHEN WORDS ARE ENTRY POINTS INTO DEEPER INQUIRY

As suggested, an entry point is any word or phrase that strikes your own subjective awareness to the point that it gives you pause. It might be:

- The **tone** in a patient's voice.
- A pronouncement delivered that contains **projected expectations or assumptions**.
- An **undercurrent of intensified feeling**, even when a feeling is being denied.
- A statement that **contradicts** an earlier statement.
- A **shifting away** from material too quickly.

To illustrate how to use words as entry points to track the therapeutic communication and delve more deeply into the hidden parts of the psyche, we have provided the following three video case illustrations for your review.

In the first case vignette, you will be introduced to a conversation between a supervisor and supervisee. The supervisee reported that an initial session with a patient appeared to be going rather successfully. However, she is uncertain "where to go from there." The supervisor helps the supervisee catch a phrase that is likely to be an entry point to gain further information about the patient's sense of self as well as her defenses as the treatment moves forward.

Please refer to the Routledge website, Video 5.1: Consultation Session on Entry Points.

Supervisee: I saw this woman who was court mandated to see me today. She had such a horrible life. At first she was suspicious of me and said she didn't want to be here. Then, she started telling me about her life circumstances, how she has three kids, and Social Services wanted her to leave her live-in boyfriend because he was an alcoholic and abusive. She said to me, "Don't they get it? If I kick him out, I don't have enough money to support the kids on my own. I keep him around because I need him to survive. I'm a survivor, you know." So, when she left, she smiled at me and said, "That wasn't as bad as I thought. You're not a snooty bitch after all." It was a great feeling. I mean, I guess that was her way of giving positive feedback. I'm not sure where I'm going to go next with her, however.

Supervisor: Maybe we can use her comment, "I'm a survivor," as an entry point for discussion in your next session. It was one statement that she made where she exhibited some "pride" in herself.

Supervisee: Yeah, you're right. But, I'm not sure how to go deeper with that comment. She said she was a survivor. What else is there to say about that?

Supervisor: Do you know what she means by survivor?

Supervisee: No, I guess not, not entirely.

Supervisor: And that's the whole point about using language as an entry point. By asking her what *she* means, you'll get more information.

	You'll go deeper. And it's a way of letting her know that you were listening to her as well. So, how might you follow-up on that?
Supervisee:	Well, I guess I can ask her what she means by survivor. But, I'm not sure where to go from there.
Supervisor:	So, some of the questions you might ask could be, "So, what's it like to be a survivor?" "How do you manage to do that day after day?" "Where do you get the energy when your boyfriend gets drunk or Social Services comes into your home?" Then, just follow her lead. What she tells you will lead you to your next question.
Supervisee:	But sometimes, when I try to go deeper with people, they shut down.
Supervisor:	Can you give me some examples of how you've tried to go deeper and the patient shuts down?
Supervisee:	I usually ask them how something makes them feel.
Supervisor:	Yes, and with people who are pretty defended or suspicious of the therapy process, asking a feeling question can be experienced as threatening, because it's too exposing of their vulnerability. It's too stimulating affectively.
Supervisee:	You're right. I see that so often. It's all about protecting themselves from feeling one-down, from feeling shame.
Supervisor:	Stay with the cognition, the language of the dialogue. If you do that, you follow where they are ready to go, where they are able to go in the present moment. Language gives us just as much information and depth as asking questions about feelings, especially in the initial phase of therapy.
Supervisee:	I get it. An entry point is a portal. That's where the story is accessible. We have to stay where the story is accessible.
Supervisor:	And that's how we learn to trust the process.

Questions for Discussion

1. In your small peer supervision group or with a colleague, discuss how your understanding of the use of entry points has been clarified.

2. Why did the supervisor focus on the patient's sense of pride as a useful first line of inquiry to delve deeper into the discussion?

3. How does the supervisor help clarify the importance of pacing the inquiry process in the interest of monitoring the patient's vulnerability?

4. Often the underbelly of pride reveals some degree of shame sensitivity. How can the supervisee be careful with the inquiry during this initial inquiry period?

In our next video case example, we see how the therapist works with a patient to shift from language to feelings. Notice what happens when the therapist uses the patient's phrase "cramped feet" to connect it to a larger dilemma involving authentic self-expression.

Please refer to the Routledge website, Video 5.2: Cramped Feet.

Questions for Review

1. Describe the word or phrase that you believe was an entry point.

2. Did you notice an intensification of tone or a shift away from hidden material?

3. Can you see how tracking the entry point of the patient's language revealed more material?

> 4. Think of your own case examples. Do you recall words or phrases that may have been entry point openings?

In our final case vignette illustrating entry points, we wish to provide an example of what can happen to the treatment relationship when the therapist misses an apparently important entry point. This vignette represents a conversation between an outside consulting psychologist who has agreed to see the patient because he is seeking help in clarifying why he is feeling "stuck" in his treatment with his current therapist.

Please refer to the Routledge website, Video 5.3: Therapeutic Impasse.

Discussion Questions

1. This patient's original therapist appeared to be using more of a cognitive-behavioral or solution-focused treatment approach. What type of slight adjustments could have been made to keep the therapy on track?

2. At what point in the treatment could the therapist have paused and started a different line of inquiry?

3. What questions might be raised that could have prevented this therapeutic impasse?

4. *The entry point phrase that the patient raised with his therapist was, "I think we're at an impasse." How does giving reassurance at this point miss deeper understanding about:*

   a. The patient's inner world and relationship patterns?

   b. His feelings of shame and failure?

   c. His reflexive protective stance toward the therapist?

MOMENT-TO-MOMENT TRACKING

Moment-to-moment tracking allows us to listen for deeper nuance in the dynamic unfolding of therapeutic conversation. By slowing the process down and remaining focused in the present, we are able to ask questions that enable us to identify a clearer picture of what constitutes internal meaning within the patient's psychic organization.

Viewed as a therapeutic technique, moment-to-moment tracking is the essence and the "glue" of therapeutic conversation. As we stay firmly focused in the present moment, a picture slowly begins to emerge, revealing where pockets of pain are deeply hidden, where early wishes and longings remain, and where over-determined efforts attempt to hide feelings of isolation, loneliness, and disenfranchisement. Gradually, we also begin to hear and see glimmers of authenticity—our patients' hopes, dreams, and fears; their innocence and unblemished decency; their raw talents and gifts.

It is only by remaining steady in this diligent and persistent tracking process that we are able to grasp how pockets of shame or feelings of inadequacy are being sequestered. Feelings of shame emerge consciously and directly only when patients have "proof" of our steadiness, proof over time that we can hold their vulnerability in ways that won't re-injure.

Re-injury can occur in various ways.

- In trying to be helpful, the therapist may attempt to offer solutions that the patient may experience as pressure, and the patient may interpret these attempts to be helpful as requiring them to move faster than they are able. Patients who have patterns of trying to please others may fall into the same trap with the therapist as evidenced in the video, "Therapeutic Impasse."
- Taking what a patient says at face value and not getting further clarification may actually leave the patient feeling *less seen* and further alone and isolated. Patients who were raised in environments that were emotionally depriving or chaotic learn that it is "normal" not to have full attention and curiosity given to them. When a therapist slows the process down to gain further understanding, the interchange becomes relationally instructive in that it affords the patient the experience of *worthiness* to take up time and space.
- If the therapist fails to make inquiries into over-determined solutions, the homeostatic defensive balance remains unchallenged. A therapist's fear of upsetting the apple cart when a patient begins to bristle around inconsistencies in behaviors or beliefs may actually set up an inadvertent collusion with the defensive posture. This is particularly true with the more grandiose presentation of narcissistic defenses.

Asking thoughtful questions can be either subtle or sometimes more pointed. Staying in the present moment and asking for clarification may enable the patient to slow their *own* process down. By further explaining what he/she believes, the patient can become more curious and self-reflective, thereby allowing for a deeper therapeutic exploration process to emerge. It is through the moment-to-moment inquiry process that we get a more complete picture of the amount of "psychic" space the over-determined idealizations occupy. In this regard, as we become better at the skill set of phenomenological or moment-to-moment tracking, we inevitably become better at overall assessment and dynamic formulation.

A way of identifying the key features of moment-to-moment tracking is to first remember that not all material is verbally revealed in the unfolding conversation. When treating individuals with narcissistic vulnerabilities, much is initially hidden from view. The therapist's task is to learn how to attend to *what is being said* and also to what is *not being said. What is not being said* begins to be exposed when the patient reveals inconsistencies in behaviors, beliefs, and expectations that are held for both self and others. Where there are inconsistencies or inequities, generally there is more to the clinical picture.

The following two case vignettes provide illustrations of phenomenological or moment-to-moment tracking. In the first case vignette, we see how the therapist uses the entry-point phrase "knee-jerk reaction of resistance" to track what is under the surface of the patient's irritation. Notice how, through persistent inquiry, the therapist patiently works with the patient's irritability and wish to shift away from his own feelings of vulnerability and inadequacy.

Please refer to the Routledge website, Video 5.4: Knee-jerk and Moment-to-Moment Tracking.

Patient: I'm getting sick to death of these long, drawn out conversations with Gloria. Something triggers "high drama" every week. She's always so wounded. She becomes wounded by something I haven't done carefully enough.

Therapist: What do you mean?

Patient: Everything. It's gotten to the point that I have a knee-jerk reaction of resistance.

Therapist: You have a knee-jerk reaction of resistance?

Patient: Yes, it's as if I'm anticipating a criticism around every corner.

Therapist: So your knee-jerk reaction is to being criticized?

Patient: It's as though I'm being tested. Then I start trying to anticipate what her next response is going to be to any answer I give.

Therapist: You start to anticipate before you offer your thoughts?

Patient: Yes. I run through two or three possibilities of how she might react to my answering something honestly. Then I try to imagine what she wants to hear from me. It's as if I need to pass some test by giving her a response that suits her, something that somehow always has to do with me providing reassurance to her. And then I start to formulate a response in opposition to that.

Therapist: So, you don't give your true response?

Patient: Well, initially no. But, now as I've been trying to watch my own thoughts, I sometimes catch myself going for an opposition response. So, I go back to seriously thinking what it is that is important to me, what I really want to say.

Therapist: So, your initial knee-jerk reaction has led you to a great deal of self-reflection. That's pretty impressive.

Patient: I suppose you're right. It's a lot better than how I used to be. But, I'm still triggered by a sense of knee-jerk panic. I've got to overcome the fear and panic that has ruled my life. (Becomes tearful) Letting go of worry is probably the most important thing to me right now. I've been imprisoned by it all my life, and I want to break free.

Therapist: Well, noticing and talking about your knee-jerk reaction is actually a step toward breaking free of the fear and panic.

Patient: What do you mean?

Therapist: You're able to observe yourself. You're able to slow yourself down enough that you don't respond from the place of panic—either in opposition or trying to please the other person. That's a step toward health. And when you do that do you notice that you are less panicked?

Patient: Yes, as a matter of fact, I am a little calmer when I sit with my thoughts and walk through the process. I never thought about it like that.

Discussion Questions

1. *Discuss how the therapist used moment-to-moment tracking to stay more closely aligned with the patient's emotional state of irritation as it is connected to his fear of being criticized.*

2. *Why is it important to track the nuances of the patient's emotional state, his desire for distance, and his fear of falling short in his partner's eyes?*

3. *What was the impact on the patient when the therapist helped to differentiate between panic and underlying feelings of shame?*

4. *How might this change the therapeutic relationship?*

5. *What impact did you see of the therapist's statement, "That's pretty impressive"?*

6. *Think of your own case examples. Are there individuals who may benefit from the process technique of moment-to-moment tracking?*

In this second video, we have provided an illustration of the "right" way and "wrong" way to proceed with moment-to-moment tracking. Please pay attention in the first video clip, "Wrong Way," to how the therapist rushes to problem solving before getting enough information. Notice the better flow in the conversation in the second video clip, "Right Way," when the therapist slows down the process and tracks the dialogue in the present moment.

Please refer to the Routledge website, Video 5.5: Wrong Way/Right Way.

Questions for Review

1. Explain why you think that the patient began to defend her husband in the first video, "Wrong Way."

2. How might the patient have interpreted the therapist's suggestion of bringing the husband in as a sign to her of rejection or unworthiness at this point in the treatment?

3. In the second video, "Right Way," point out the tracking points that helped the patient shift into deeper conversation about her own life and her mother's messages around worthiness.

4. Why was it important for the therapist to distinguish between the feelings of loneliness and feelings of unworthiness?

5. How might that become a breakthrough in the treatment?

Here is a list of summary points that capture the power of moment-to-moment tracking as a process intervention in dynamic therapies.

- Listening is a circular and systemic process. As therapists, we listen best through tracking, but it is important to point out that neither tracking nor listening is linear or sequential.
- The Four Quadrant Model itself is seen as circular and systemic, where the therapist may subtly "telegraph" any quadrant if the situation permits, without following any particular order.
- Part of how we achieve the circular fluidity that the model illustrates is to stay as closely immersed in the present as possible.
- Our aim in staying in the phenomenological present is to go deeper, to apprehend a fuller context, and thereby immerse ourselves in the more complete understanding of the patient's subjective experience.
- The use of entry points is a therapeutic opportunity to delve into the phenomenological tracking process.
- Our attention to process increases in importance as we pay attention to the micro-level of our patients' subjective experience in any given moment.
- Phenomenological process is elevated over content. The meaning-making connections between part *and* whole become more available to us the more we are empathically immersed in the present.
- Stated otherwise, rather than rushing to interpret and thereby imposing the therapist's meaning prematurely, the moment-to-moment inquiry process in the present allows for greater degrees of attunement.

As we can see, tracking the therapeutic dialogue slows the process down and opens the doorway to deeper inquiry. This is how unconscious or dissociated material becomes conscious and integrated into the personality. It becomes a vehicle for how the patient's learned style of attachment can change from insecure to more secure and become anchored in the patient's authentic self.

FORECASTING

Our final therapeutic technique, forecasting, can perhaps best be described as long-term excavation work. Initially, it requires tuning into patient material that is defensively based, under the surface, or actively denied. Much like slowing down the process, forecasting can be readily integrated into most approaches to treatment (in general, this is true of all the process interventions we are recommending in this chapter). One way of understanding the technique of forecasting is to see it as seed planting—using words or phrases that plant a seed—or food for thought for deeper exploration when the time is right.

In other words, forecasting acts as a subliminal introduction to material that the patient may not be ready to acknowledge consciously at any given moment of the treatment.

- Forecasting is often used early in the treatment of addictive disorders. For example, if a patient says, "I can't deal with people who are losers," a forecasting response might be, "Is it easier to not focus on things that are irritating?" This use of forecasting sets the stage for eventually discussing the broader defense of denial.
- It is also used when the therapist senses that the patient is developing a readiness for a breakthrough of insight, penetrating the once-held homeostatic defense mechanisms. For example, if a patient begins to voice irritation around a parent's continual requests for attention, the therapist may introduce the topic of loyalty as a way of seed planting.
- Forecasting is done by having the therapist casually mention a word or phrase that raises into consciousness a concept or idea that may yet be too *hot to handle*. For example, introducing the taboo word or phrase is a way of normalizing a taboo subject or subliminally giving permission to the patient to think and talk about forbidden subject matter that was formerly shameful or dangerous.

As we become more familiar with the Four Quadrant Model, we begin to develop a sense about which quadrant material is being defended against based on reactions that appear to hit a nerve or are too hot to handle. The patient's initial reactivity can gradually become neutralized as the therapist subtly gives permission for the patient to question beliefs, fear, or assumptions. Alternatively, the therapist may raise questions about the patient's assumptions around what it means to be loyal, worthy, or a good person. By examining the *intensity of over-determined efforts* through using the technique of forecasting, the patient will gradually begin to see how these efforts compromise healthier aspects of living, such as the quality of the person's relationships or the maintenance of self-care.

HOW CAN FORECASTING BE USED?

Forecasting facilitates our ability to connect psychic parts to a whole. Forecasting can be used to create a leverage point into deeper inquiry, as illustrated through the following examples.

- When there is a conscious over-reliance on Quadrant One, it is likely that the patient has difficulty handling vulnerability or fears of inadequacy. In this instance, asking a question such as, "Are you comfortable relying on others?" opens a doorway into curiosity as to a possible imbalance between Quadrant One and Quadrant Three.

- If the patient becomes defensive or avoids this initial "forecasting question," the therapist might do well to then wonder about how the patient handles disappointments and loss. This introduces a conversation about the relationship between Quadrant One and Quadrant Three. We see how over-determined efforts to achieve on one's own needs are reinforced within the context of relationships. Do people notice the patient's efforts or give praise? What happens when others do not notice?

- An example that reveals connections to Quadrant Two might be to inquire into the patient's minimization of the overuse of substances to calm anxiety, or the lack of concern about too little sleep. The therapist can use questions around generic self-care and limitation as a way of introducing or "forecasting" a concern about the cost of over-determined strategies to achieve success. In this way, the word "success" becomes the forecasting leverage point into hidden material.

- As a final example that can uncover material from Quadrant Four, if the patient subtly devalues others yet wonders why he or she has difficulty maintaining relationships, the therapist can begin to use "forecasting language" that randomly introduces the idea of *getting even*, *testing the relationship*, *or thinking of revenge*. Another access point is to ask the patient what happens when he or she experiences feelings of disappointment.

FORECASTING AND TIMING OF THERAPEUTIC INTERVENTIONS

A therapist may introduce a forecasting question or statement even though the therapist may know that the patient *may not be ready* to hear the information or question. Even if the patient initially disagrees with what the therapist is suggesting, this does not mean that the intervention failed. Forecasting is the ability to trust that when the therapist plants a seed, that seed will eventually be remembered and take root. Once articulated, the therapist can come back to the word or phrase that forecasts a future need for self-reflection, curiosity, and reorganization, as the patient develops more of an emotional readiness.

An example of this might be around the issue of safety. Let us say that the patient has a history of traumatic abuse, coupled with a distant and withholding mother. A forecasting technique would be to inquire about issues of safety in a general sense and then wonder if there are perhaps times when the patient feels less safe. Although the patient may not be ready to discuss safety if the dissociative split is too great, continuing to wonder about safety whenever the content material permits is a type of seed planting that will bear eventual fruit.

When the patient complains about her mother, we could wonder what the *overall* relationship was like when she was small—did she feel safe or protected by her mother?

When there is history of trauma, we know that issues of safety and trust lie just beneath the surface. Since our clinical margin of safety with trauma and abuse will indeed be small, steps will inevitably be cautiously taken.

The timing or readiness to acknowledge the pain that attends a history of trauma can often rest on the effective use of forecasting. As with any other technique, experience is our best teacher.

In the next two video case vignettes, we have provided further examples of forecasting as an intervention technique. In the first video, the therapist forecasts the idea of fear and safety as it might coalesce around the patient's own measure of challenging herself by being attracted to men who live on the edge. Notice how the patient's sense of pride is measured by how successful she is in handling dangerous situations although the conscious awareness of danger is not registered or named as a situation that may be frightening or fearful.

Please refer to the Routledge website, Video 5.6: Forecasting and Buried Trauma.

Patient: I've always been attracted to racy men, men who live on the edge.
Therapist: What do you mean racy and on the edge?
Patient: Men who weren't boring, men who were a challenge.
Therapist: A challenge? In what way?
Patient: Men that were so sure of themselves that they felt they could conquer the world.
Therapist: And how do you find that challenging?
Patient: Well, it was a test and measure of my own strength as well. I took pride in testing myself to see if I could keep up with them. I wasn't afraid of their intellect. I never am.
Therapist: Were you afraid of *anything* about them?
Patient: What do you mean? I said it was a challenge that I found engaging.
Therapist: I know, but you mentioned what you *weren't* afraid of their intellect. I was just curious if there were any situations where these challenges put you in a tight or uncomfortable spot.
Patient: Oh, you mean like with my ex-husband. Yes, that was a grueling divorce. I don't know why I didn't see his dark side underneath that charm. I guess I'm a bad judge of character. I keep picking these men who later surprise me with their dark side. It's a pattern.
Therapist: It's almost as if you don't register when a situation might be dangerous or unsafe.
Patient: Unsafe? I never thought about that before. Safety? No one ever talked to me about this in terms of paying attention to safety. This

never came up in my prior therapies. I always thought it was a good thing to take pride in being able to fend for myself.

Therapist: I'm sure that this was true. But sometimes when we have had to learn to fend for ourselves, we have to also learn to block out cues of danger—situations or people where things might not feel that safe.

Patient: Yes, my childhood certainly couldn't be described as safe. There was so much chaos. But I never connected *that* to what made me attracted to the men I have picked.

Therapist: As you look back on it now, can you see where there may have been red flags indicating danger, small signs that you may have ignored?

Patient: Well, not at the time, but now that you mention it, I suppose there were some quirky things that I noticed about both of my husbands that I said weren't important.

Therapist: By telling yourself to ignore dangerous things, calling them unimportant, is that how you might have missed signals that could let you know when someone might not feel completely safe?

Questions for Discussion

1. What was the patient's reaction to the therapist's initial use of the word "unsafe"?

2. How did the therapist use the word to forecast curiosity and encourage the patient to take issues of safety more seriously?

3. What was your sense about the timing of this intervention?

4. Where might the therapist go next?

In this second video case example, the issue of relational loyalty is gently challenged. Here the therapist is using the technique of forecasting to uncover unconscious material in Quadrant Three.

Please refer to the Routledge website, Video 5.7: Forecasting and Loyalty.

Therapist: Last week you were telling me about your mother, how she stayed with your father regardless of how much he drank. I know that you were very upset when you left the session, so I wanted to follow-up with what got triggered.

Patient: I find that when we talk about this, I get so *mad* at my mother. How could she be so stupid, so weak? Then I start to feel guilty for thinking bad thoughts about it. She had no choice after all. She only had a high school education and had to raise four kids.

Therapist: So you get mad, then you start to feel guilty. Does your anger reflect some way of being disloyal to your mother?

Patient: Maybe. It's like my anger is not honoring her sacrifice for us kids.

Therapist: I see. If you feel anger or frustration toward your mother for taking your father's abuse, you immediately feel disloyal because she stayed with him because of you and your siblings?

Patient: Are you saying that she stayed for other reasons?

Therapist: I don't know, but I was just trying to be open and curious about other reasons she may have stayed.

Patient: Hm. Let me think about that. (Pause) Maybe, she really loved him. When he wasn't drinking, he wasn't a bad guy, kind of sweet actually.

Therapist: So, your mother had a loyalty to your father. She was loyal to the part of him that was sweet. And then, that meant she was able to ignore the parts of him that came home drunk and physically abused her?

Patient: I guess so. Pretty stupid, isn't it?

Therapist: So, your mother never got angry or frustrated with your father?

Patient: No, she was too afraid.

Therapist: Just out of curiosity, when you found yourself getting angry with your mother last week, did you feel that you were being disloyal? If I understand you correctly, your mother was never disloyal to your father because she didn't or couldn't express her anger. But, I'm just wondering, if you find yourself feeling angry, is that why you suddenly feel guilty—like you did something your mother taught you never to do?

Questions for Discussion

1. How does the therapist plant an initial seed of curiosity about loyalty issues by referring back to the previous session without mentioning the patient's affect?

---

2. How might this have enabled the patient to bring up her own feelings of anger and then volunteer how she experienced guilt afterwards?

3. Discuss how the therapist links anger, guilt, and loyalty as a means of forecasting or opening a doorway to further exploration of the loyalty contract in her family of origin.

4. When the therapist challenges the notion of sacrifice and loyalty by asking if there were other reasons that her mother might have stayed with her father, how does that begin to loosen the grip of the old loyalty contract?

5. Discuss how the therapist then uses forecasting (linking loyalty with a dissociative split) to further expand the patient's curiosity about her own authentic feelings.

SUMMARY OF LISTENING, TRACKING, AND INTERVENTION TECHNIQUES

When we become more adept at listening and tracking the therapeutic dialogue, it empowers the therapist to process information in a way that reveals how various parts of the psyche are connected and dependent on one another. The Four Quadrant Model illustrates how each part or quadrant of the psyche is tightly woven and interconnected to comprise a homeostatic balance within the personality.

When we are better able to anticipate what might be missing from the picture at any given moment, we become more confident in our ability to anticipate what it takes to stay with the unfolding therapeutic process. We are able to assess the timing of interventions more adeptly if we can understand what might occur to the homeostatic balance, such as when we attempt to alter a part of the personality matrix too early without understanding how it comprises the larger whole.

6

The Dissociative Spectrum

[It] is most often not what we don't know about ourselves, but what we both know and don't know, the ways in which certain things we "know" do not really influence very much what we do or what we feel.

—Wachtel (2008, p. 143)

Parental behavior that produces disorganization within the child's mind thus may create not only an impairment in the functioning in the moment, but, if repeated, a tendency to dis-integrate in the future. Such a form of self-dysregulation may be at the heart of dissociation.

—Siegel (2003, p. 33)

Despite early references in the literature to dissociation, the spectrum of dissociative processes has not been well understood. As a result, our understanding of the issues of shame and narcissistic disturbances has been delayed, misunderstood, or thought to be untreatable. Thereby, inroads into the treatment of trauma, affect dysregulation, and various forms of addiction have largely been under-treated within psychodynamic paradigms.

However, interest in dissociative mechanisms within the analytic community never dropped out of sight completely, as evidenced through the contributions of Horney (1939, 1945, 1950), Ferenczi (1926, 1994), and Kohut (1966, 1977, 1984). More recently, our understanding has been deepened through the contributions of Bernstein and Putnam (1986), Courtois and Ford (2009), Howell (2005), Levine (2010, 2015), Liotti (1992, 1999), Main (1995), Spiegel (1990), Stern (1985, 1997), and Wachtel (2008), among others.

Putnam (1985) explains that the range of dissociative experiences can include depersonalization, amnesia, and the subjective sense of alternative identity states. As well, he notes that more overtly observable phenomena such as changes in facial and/or vocal expression and trance states are often associated with more extreme states of dissociation, as in dissociative identity disorder and fugue states.

Traumatic events in childhood and severe episodic episodes of trauma in adulthood can trigger various states of dissociation. Peter Levine (2015) states, "Trauma shocks the brain, stuns the mind, and freezes the body" (p. xxi). He encourages therapists to move toward an integrated approach to treating trauma, reminding us that traumatic memories can imprint in the body, brain, and mind, as well as the psyche and soul.

Dissociative Continuum

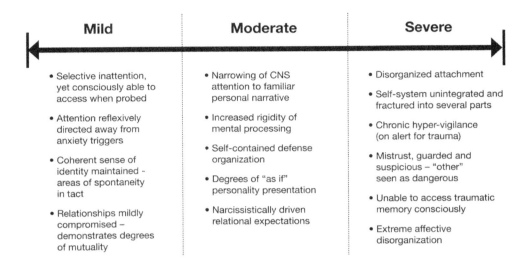

Mild	Moderate	Severe
• Selective inattention, yet consciously able to access when probed	• Narrowing of CNS attention to familiar personal narrative	• Disorganized attachment
• Attention reflexively directed away from anxiety triggers	• Increased rigidity of mental processing	• Self-system unintegrated and fractured into several parts
• Coherent sense of identity maintained - areas of spontaneity in tact	• Self-contained defense organization	• Chronic hyper-vigilance (on alert for trauma)
• Relationships mildly compromised - demonstrates degrees of mutuality	• Degrees of "as if" personality presentation	• Mistrust, guarded and suspicious – "other" seen as dangerous
	• Narcissistically driven relational expectations	• Unable to access traumatic memory consciously
		• Extreme affective disorganization

Figure 6.1 Dissociative Continuum

It is important to emphasize that the defense mechanism of dissociation can encompass varying degrees of intensity, frequency, and duration. All points on the dissociative spectrum involve splitting off dystonic aspects of reality from conscious awareness and behavior. When viewed on a continuum, Howell (2005) states that we are better able to understand the subtle nuances of dissociation as states that often occur in the "normal" population, not just in severe psychopathology. Dissociative splitting is a form of disavowal, something that is disconnected from conscious awareness at any given time. The greater the dissociative process, the deeper the level of trauma and underlying shame is likely to be.

The following graphic illustrates the spectrum of dissociative process. Note that the continuum moves from mild to severe, with specific descriptors to help the therapist track both micro-dissociative episodes moment-to-moment as well as more entrenched dissociative conditions that compromise broader areas of patient functioning.

THE SPECTRUM OF DISSOCIATION AS IT RELATES TO SHAME

Dissociation, shame, and trauma are heavily interactive and interpersonally bound. Where you see signs of dissociation in the present moment, generally some trigger of shame or trauma has been activated. As a therapist, you may not be immediately aware of what has been triggered, as the trigger may be dissociated from the patient's conscious awareness as well. Crastnopol (2015) has made the important point that micro-dissociative situations "can be hidden in plain sight—being wounded or betrayed emotionally by one's earliest significant others during infancy and childhood can create a sequestered doubt that poses a formidable resistance to creating generative bonds later in life. And micro-traumatic moments may be part of the texture of those early hurts" (pp. 3–4).

Some therapists are less familiar with the theoretical underpinnings of how micro-dissociative moments occur within any given session. They can miss the fact that non-conscious or semi-conscious affective triggers are at play more frequently than earlier theory and training led us to believe. Observers of parent-infant research have helped us understand how disorganized and insecure attachments often replicate themselves around affect or relational ruptures or misattunements. The implication of this in terms of therapeutic listening and moment-to-moment tracking is significant both in terms of catching dissociative ruptures as they occur within the treatment hour as well as helping establish a more securely attached therapeutic bond.

How can we assess when a patient comes to us with pronounced but dissociated feelings of shame? The following pieces of information taken from a patient's history indicate that there are likely underlying feelings of shame. The greater the likelihood of shame, the greater likelihood that dissociative mechanisms will eventually surface. Diagnostic indicators are as follows:

- The patient has a history of trauma or abuse.
- Parental attachments were insecure or disorganized.
- Physical and psychological safety was compromised.
- A sense of personal value was measured by "what I can produce" rather than "who I am."
- Performance standards and expectations from parental figures were harsh, unrealistic, or narcissistically driven.

RECOGNIZING DISSOCIATIVE PROCESS AS IT UNFOLDS WITHIN THE TREATMENT

How can we recognize when dissociative processes are occurring? Below is a partial list of *types* of micro-dissociations, followed by an accompanying example of what a patient might say to telegraph that a dissociative communication has just occurred.

- The patient can cognitively report a humiliating event from childhood but cannot capture its affective strength: *"I just decided not to think about it."*

- The patient experiences powerful affective reactions (nightmares, hyper-arousal, sudden panic), but the emotions do not connect with any recognizable content: *"I suddenly get overwhelmed with a terrible fear, but I don't know what it is."*
- Both content and affect are dissociated from awareness. The patient can present with disconnected strands of bodily symptoms (nausea, choking) or blandness: *"There's nothing there; I don't know what to say."*
- The patient has moments of being able to connect with the cognitive content and also separately with the affective component but cannot experience them *together*. When one part of the whole is in awareness, the other part drops out of awareness, and this can occur even within the same session. *"I don't remember. Did I just say that? I don't remember saying that."*

From a relational viewpoint, dissociation is an attempt to maintain a sense of safety and stability; that is, a valiant effort to preserve the tenuous bond of attachment. The price for that attachment often means dissociating from important pieces of reality or important feeling states in order to preserve the precarious bond. As well, some level of dissociation can also occur following a movement toward authenticity when the insight triggers a flashback-like experience of the original psychological insult.

Levine (2015) believes that traumatically induced dissociative triggers can be treated by attending to a form of *physiological tracking of traumatic procedural memory*. The tracking of procedural memories involves attending to *movement patterns* that include learned motor skills, automatic responses of approach/avoidance, and instinctual survival triggers that generally override other implicit and explicit memory subtypes (p. 38). Whereas a psychodynamically oriented therapist might attend to micro-dissociative episodes that threaten the patient's sense of *presentness and relational connection* in the moment, Levine encourages us to also attend to idiosyncratic micro-movements that may capture a "body memory" of trauma without it ever surfacing into conscious awareness. His approach on a neurophysiological level is to help the patient move from immobility and helplessness, to hyperarousal and mobilization, and finally to integration and mastery of the truncated, repressed memory system (p. 51).

TRACKING DISSOCIATIVE PROCESS

When the therapist senses that a micro- or macro-dissociative episode may have occurred in the unfolding treatment, the next step is to pause and ask, "What just happened?" Generally, if the therapist can articulate to the patient the fact that some form of rupture just occurred, a shared conscious awareness then can begin to develop.

Like any other form of listening and attending, the therapist brings awareness in noticing the subtle shifts or nuances in conversation, as well as attending to more abrupt shifts that occur in the dialogic exchange. Both of these are an indication that some level of dissociation has occurred.

When tracking dissociation specifically, it is important to pay attention to:

- Episodes of remembering and forgetting.
- A rapid shifting away from or minimizing of affect.
- Abrupt disconnection from conversation, followed by reconnection and reengagement in the present.

As stated, such tracking is important because it helps raise the dissociative dynamic into conscious awareness. Thus, palpating the dissociation in that moment, through observation and questioning, the patient may eventually be able to catch a fleeting thought or feeling and report it. If the therapist is able to link a prior verbal cue with the affective dissociative trigger, gradually the patient's self-reflective capacities can begin to also work in the service of accessing implicit memories that have been triggered. As micro-dissociations become more visible, they slowly begin to be integrated.

Clinical awareness of micro-dissociations is always contextually rooted and thus lends itself more easily to moment-to-moment tracking. Awareness and acknowledgment can assist in bringing more dissociative processes into a relational "holding experience." As a result, the often elusive quality of a dissociative split can come into focus.

Thus, when the therapists reflects back to patients that a micro-dissociation has occurred, patients can then gradually become more connected to their own experience of coming in and out of dissociation. As trust grows in the intersubjective moment, the therapeutic alliance itself gradually begins to change, reflecting the patient's growth in self-reflective capacities.

If the therapist does not engage in a relational posture in the present moment, what often happens is that the patient is left with an experiential *rupture* that can be best articulated by a patient's comment, "There are no words to describe what just happened to me." Elevating experiential process over cognitive content allows the therapist to catch micro-dissociations that in turn can cut through deep-seated feelings of isolation. This then deepens the immediate level of empathic immersion in the here and now.

EXAMPLES OF DISSOCIATE PROCESS: THREE VIDEO CASE VIGNETTES

The following three video case vignettes feature examples of the broad scope of dissociative process that can manifest within the treatment exchange. The first vignette illustrates more severe and pervasive dissociative process. The second case vignette highlights how initial gains within the treatment may also trigger an episode of dissociative activity. The third case vignette provides an illustration of what happens when the therapist tracks the inconsistencies around the patient's newly experienced sense of self-confidence that has not yet been integrated.

In the first video case vignette, we see a young woman with "memory impairment" (dissociative episodes) often triggered by intensity of affective experience. At first the patient forgets what occurred on a feeling level; then she is able to retrieve the memory at the cost of any affective experience being retained. This is especially true with feelings of exuberance, joy, or excitement on her own behalf. The woman's history includes growing up in a Midwestern town with Evangelical parents who were very strict, intrusive, and punishing when any of their six children deviated from core religious beliefs. This was true around any expression of sexual curiosity, dating relationships, or the press for adolescent individuation and personal freedom. Corporal punishment was often used when children "misbehaved."

A year into the treatment (much later than when this vignette was recorded), the patient began to remember more of her childhood memories that had heretofore been blocked. She was able to remember a painful and traumatic episode that occurred when the patient was sixteen. Dating a boy in high school (in secret), she discovered that she was pregnant. Terrified to let her parents know, she agreed to have her boyfriend's family arrange for an abortion. Later, when her parents discovered what had happened, the patient's father severely abused her physically, disowned her, and kicked her out of the house. The patient later moved to New York where she made attempts to work as an actress. Anxiety and increasing lapses in memory and confusion are what brought her into treatment.

In this case vignette, relatively early in the treatment, you see the therapist gently working with pervasive feelings of shame and fear, as the patient attempts to cover up her overcompensation by wishing that other people would forget or not notice her forgetfulness. This indicates a partial awareness of her dissociative process as it relates to the retention of memory. However, she is unable to link the affective triggers that initiate episodes of forgetting. By providing reassurance and asking if these episodes occurred within the session, the therapist is able to direct the patient toward the therapeutic holding environment of safety. When this occurs, we see that the patient is able to access and reveal more of her history around parental upbringing, including the expression of negative feeling states.

Please refer to the Routledge website, Video 6.1: Severe Dissociation.

Questions for Review

1. Notice what occurs when the therapist repeats the patient's phrase, "Half dead and half alive."

a. How do you understand the patient's irritation with the therapist?

b. What do you think the patient is telegraphing when she says, "I don't want to waste any time"?

2. Early in the segment, the patient begins to explain her process of "forgetting." She gets excited about something, and then it gets lost. When she remembers, the excitement seems to have diminished.

a. Dynamically and affectively, what might you speculate is going on in this dissociation and recovery process?

b. What function does the excitement going flat have on the patient's attempts at homeostatic regulation?

c. What function might the flatness have on revealing aspects of "loyalty binds"?

3. Why do you think that the therapist then asked, "Does that happen in here?"

a. How might directing the patient into the therapeutic relationship help her better track micro-dissociations in the present moment?

b. What does this question in turn reveal about the relational dynamics and the patient's internal state?

4. When the patient admits to things going "dead," she becomes angry and justifies herself by explaining that she's not doing this on purpose.

a. What does this statement reveal about her early childhood relationships?

b. How does this sequence provide an entry into exploring feelings of shame more directly?

c. What further questions might you ask to access feelings of shame?

5. What do you make of the therapist providing immediate reassurance and making the connection that positive feelings also seem to fade first?

6. Notice that the positive reframe evokes a more extreme dissociative reaction followed by further triggers of shame.

In the second case vignette in this chapter, we have provided a review of micro-dissociation as it pertains to other concepts introduced thus far. In this consultation session, Jack and Patricia are discussing how the Four Quadrant Model can be used not only in the service of seeing how parts of the psyche connect to other parts and the larger whole, but also how the model can be used to more accurately capture when micro-dissociations occur within a session.

Please refer to the Routledge website, Video 6.2: Part-Whole Analysis and Micro-Dissociation.

Questions for Review

1. How do you understand the circularity of the model as it can be used in identifying how parts of the psyche are either connected or disconnected from one another?

2. *Tracking the shifts in affect as a means of using the Four Quadrant Model systemically is a vehicle for seeing how and when micro-dissociations occur moment-to-moment.*

    a. *How would attending to shifts that occur within the dialogue allow you greater ease into noticing the micro-dissociations as they unfold?*

    b. *What kind of precedent might you start to build if you noticed "out loud" what just happened?*

3. *When the therapist comments on these affective shifts occurring, how might this also increase the patient's conscious awareness of dissociative breaks over time?*

4. *How does this build affective attunement and more secure relational attachment between the therapist and patient?*

5. *Discuss what the supervisors mean by "tracking in the present allows the past to be revealed organically."*

In this third case vignette, Patricia and Jack are working with a supervisee who begins by describing gains she has made with a patient around affect-regulation and trust. However, this therapeutic progress is now coupled with the therapist experiencing moments of *feeling stuck* when the patient becomes triggered by intense feelings of rage that send her into a dissociative state. The patient, herself, feels *stuck* in early, pre-verbal memories of pain, isolation, and fear. In this clinical situation, the patient is triggered into episodes of dissociation when the sheer intensity of affect interrupts her ability to access her "thinking brain" to help her self-soothe and modulate feelings of deep pain and despair.

Please refer to the Routledge website, Video 6.3: Consultation Session on Using the Therapeutic Relationship to Interrupt Dissociative Process.

Questions for Discussion

1. In the beginning of this vignette, the supervisee is describing gains the patient has made around dissociative process. The patient is able to identify a part of herself that is the child, and she is often able to have a conversation with that part of herself when alone. However, the therapist describes moments where she, herself feels stuck in her ability to help the patient. Discuss how you might understand the "stuckness" as:

   a. The patient's inability to access relational connection when she is experiencing a dissociative episode.

   b. A wish for the therapist to do something to magically fix the situation.

   c. Being "trapped" within a body memory that freezes the patient, involuntarily triggering a dissociative state.

2. How is the supervisee somewhat drawn into this wish as a reflection of feeling stuck?

3. Discuss your thoughts about Jack's suggestion around joining the patient in her stuckness and declaring that openly in the dialogue.

4. The supervisee describes the patient's stuckness as "a profound sense of abandonment, grief, and fear," where the patient goes to a place of pre-verbal panic and constriction.

a. Why do you think Patricia asked the question, "Is she aware of your presence in the room?"

b. How might this be a barometer for assessing the patient's level of dissociation?

5. According to Bessel van der Kolk (2014), when you can engage a patient in physical movement of any kind, it allows for a break in the dissociative process.

a. How might something as simple as making eye contact break a dissociative episode?

b. Making eye contact helps bring the patient back into the room in the present moment. Explain how this can help strengthen the therapeutic bond and foster a more secure attachment.

c. Explain how making eye contact or engaging the patient in physical movement may cut through feelings and body memories of complete abandonment?

d. Explain how this can begin to help build further gains around modulation of affect.

e. Explain how this can begin to ameliorate feelings of hopelessness and despair.

SUMMARY: DISSOCIATIVE PROCESS

Tracking dissociative ruptures within the session affords us a window into fleeting affective triggers or memory traces that often go unnoticed (the process can occur in day-to-day conversations as well). Becoming attuned to these micro-ruptures allows the therapist the following understanding:

- Help in making sense out of contradictory pieces of information from patients.
- Help in assessing rigidity of beliefs.
- Help in understanding the mechanism of dissociation as an attempt at affect-regulation, keeping painful feelings of shame outside of conscious awareness.
- Help in tracking when behaviors and beliefs don't match, thus increasing our understanding of the patient's compulsively driven organizing schemas.

By referring to the Four Quadrant Model to see which quadrants may be at play, we can begin to bring curiosity and conscious awareness into the present moment, the moment where the dissociative rupture occurs. Viewed in a non-linear and fluid way, the Four Quadrant Model can alter how we make connections between the psychological past and the psychological present.

The ways in which we listen to the unfolding narrative of our patients' lives and engage relationally are *intrinsically* linked. For example, if we believe that material the patient presents within a session is merely a reenactment of past hurts or fixations, our listening attention will be skewed toward finding static connections between the patient's dialogue and instinctual past. This runs the risk of missing nuances of micro-change, including the process changes in behaviors or beliefs based on *any* given context.

We have suggested that micro-dissociations occur in a dynamic, fluid, and non-linear way. Thus, if we maintain a posture grounded in the understanding that unfinished historical material will become manifest since it is still *alive* in the present, our ability to let the dynamic process unfold in front of us becomes much easier.

Unwrapping the Complexities of the Treatment of Shame

Each type of micro-trauma is underwritten by its own admixture of narcissistic self-investment, hostility, envy, indifference, anxiety, or shame.
—Crastnopol (2015, p. 8)

Denial occurs when one is ashamed of being ashamed. Under these conditions, shame becomes recursive and self-perpetuating. Unacknowledged shame builds a wall between persons and between groups. A chain reaction occurs, shame building on shame.
—Scheff and Retzinger (1991, pp. 29–30)

Th[e] collapse of the implicit self is signaled by the amplification of the affects of shame and disgust, and by the cognitions of hopelessness and helplessness. Because the right hemisphere mediates the communication and regulation of emotional states, the rupture of intersubjectivity is accompanied by an instant dissipation of safety and trust, a common occurrence in the treatment of the right brain deficits of severe personality disorders.
—Schore (2011, p. 81)

THE SECRETS OF SHAME

Shame sits front and center in the visual graphic of the Four Quadrant Model. As therapists, the importance of understanding the powerful grip that shame has on our patients is foundational to effective experience-near treatment. When we attune our ear toward the nuances of shame or shame derivatives, we deepen our compassion around patient attempts to disconnect from shameful feelings through narcissistic displays of overcompensation, grandiosity, self-loathing, or even the wish to strike out in retaliation. As Patricia DeYoung (2015) states, "When clients finally speak of the pain and destruction that shame wreaks in their lives, they often ask, 'Can anything make this better?' I often respond, 'Shame needs light and air' " (p. 116).

However, in the early years of analytic practice, shame was only acknowledged on the perimeters of the psychodynamic process. Shame was not viewed as integral to resolving the feelings of guilt that stemmed from early infantile longings. For the most part, shame was seen as a derivative of guilt and therefore considered to be secondary in treatment. A theory of shame and trauma had not yet evolved to allow for the possibility that guilt could conversely be seen as a derivative of shame. And yet, shame has been a preoccupation of humankind for millennia.

Although unacknowledged earlier in the field's development, shame has recently become more recognized in the mental health field. We could say that the acknowledgment has almost forced itself on us through rapid advances in the treatment of trauma. Progress in the treatment of trauma enabled practitioners to see the extent of damage done to the psyche when insecure attachment or traumatic breaches of safety interfere with healthy development. As a result, therapists are becoming more optimistic that focusing upon the treatment of shame and shame derivatives can produce positive results.

In this chapter, as a way of beginning our exploration of shame, we want to reiterate that the Four Quadrant Model provides a systemic template from which therapists can begin to understand the close connection between narcissistic defenses and the often dissociated feelings of shame, self-hate, and despair. In the previous chapter, we explored the dissociative spectrum as it pertained to trauma and insecure attachments. When we are dealing with various levels of trauma, shifting our therapeutic attention to shame allows us to "hear" defensive overcompensations more quickly and more easily. As well, it allows us to more readily "see" the connection between trauma, attachment styles, and shame. This is the essence of part-whole analysis.

Understanding the grip that shame has on the psyche allows the therapist to appreciate how difficult it is to uncover, track, and eventually dismantle feelings of shame and humiliating distress. The following statements present foundational "truths" about shame and psychic organization:

- Narcissism is the ultimate attempt to avoid shame.
- The direct experience of shame poses a psychic threat.
- Unacknowledged shame is what connects the parts of the injured self to a whole.
- Shame activates secrecy in an attempt to hide one's psychic vulnerability.
- Once begun, the secrecy builds on itself, paradoxically creating further depths of increasingly hidden shame.
- Shame can be understood as a hidden belief of "this is who I really am." Thus, the secret belief continues to fuel narcissistically driven attempts at overcompensation.
- Grandiose overcompensations function to hide a secret part of the self that somehow feels defective, no matter how successful the compensation appears.
- Moment-to-moment tracking is a method to gradually examine and expose underlying shame through dismantling over-determined standards and through questioning inconsistencies in behavior.

- The tendency of the therapist to avoid looking at shame directly has to do, in part, with the psychological weight and toll that holding this painful emotion of our patients takes on the therapist. Indeed, shame can have a marked contagion effect, leaving the therapist at greater risk for burnout.
- The ability to sit with our patients as this emotion comes to the surface requires considerable skill as well as personal reflection and psychotherapy so that the therapist's own shame triggers are minimized.

As we develop more of an "ear" for listening for undercurrents of shame, it is also important to identify behaviors and beliefs that patients present to us that actually *mask* feelings of shame. Individuals with narcissistic vulnerabilities can self-protectively overcompensate in the following ways:

- Bragging, puffing oneself up, needing to be right.
- Excessive efforts to please others.
- Putting other people down or expecting the worst from others.
- Disinvolvement, fatalism, passivity, resignation.
- Extreme standards and demands for perfection.
- Belief in absolute answers and demands for proof.

These identifying features help the therapist more easily recognize "the tip of the iceberg" of various entry points, both behavioral and linguistic, often associated with hidden feelings of shame. Each of the above examples offers a different picture or *type* of narcissistic solution. Often the grandiose type is most popularized, and thus is the most easily recognized form of narcissistic overcompensation. However, the overly pleasing, self-effacing position, as well as the resigned position, as exemplified by disinvolvement or passive defeat, also represent equally prevalent styles of narcissistic character solutions.

ACCESSING HIDDEN FEELINGS OF SHAME

Often when therapists get "stuck" in the treatment, we have found that there has been an under-attention to one of the quadrants. This under-attention may be, in part, a way that therapists have unwittingly colluded to avoid contact with shame. Not infrequently, therapists are uncertain as to how to broach feelings of underlying shame out of the often legitimate fear of causing premature exposure and thus intensifying deeper feelings of shame. Fear and confusion can contribute to the field's avoidance or "blind spots" in acknowledging the power that shame has had over the psyche.

The Four Quadrant Model is meant to help the therapist gently ease into the penetration of shame by moving around the four aspects of psychic presentation, as they each manifest within the treatment situation. The circular working of the quadrants, layer by layer, is much like peeling an onion. Each penetration becomes a connection that leads to further integration, thus creating a "sturdier" psychic scaffolding. And once this relational scaffolding is experienced between the patient and the therapist, the ability to hold painful feelings of shame more directly becomes possible.

In this opening vignette to our chapter on shame, we find a woman who is in the middle of a long-term therapy process. She has made significant gains in the arena of self-esteem and self-awareness, including questioning family members as to memories that are beginning to surface around early childhood abuse. Here, she had an emergency call, having been thrown into an emotional tailspin. Feelings of shame and self-loathing come to the surface as she is actively being challenged by her boyfriend. This is a case example where the capacity for self-reflection, accompanied by memory triggers of abuse, *can quickly turn against the self*. In this session, pay attention to how the therapist works with containing feelings of shame, encouraging the patient not to turn these feelings against herself.

Please refer to the Routledge website, Video 7.1: Quieting Shame and Self-Hate.

Questions for Discussion

1. *Identify three to four messages of containment that the therapist communicates to the patient in the first minutes of this vignette to help calm the reactivation of the patient's shame triggers.*

2. *How do you think this initial containing/soothing stance impacts the course of the remainder of the session?*

3. *What impact does the therapist's empathy, expressed in her sorrow for the patient's feelings of shame, have in reinforcing recent therapeutic gains and validating the patient's growing sense of authenticity?*

---

4. Discuss what effect the therapist saying, "Wait a minute," might have on helping the patient differentiate between the content of relational feedback being given to her and how someone delivers feedback.

5. When the therapist brings up the possibility of the patient's boyfriend being threatened by her recent gains, discuss the systemic impact shame, including shame sensitivity and recovery from shame, might have on the relational homeostatic balance.

6. Identify when the patient shifts from regaining her strength and memory around recent events that might "level the playing field of the relationship," and then again returns to self-blame.

   a. What function does returning to self-denigration have at this time in the therapeutic exchange?

   b. How does the therapist manage the patient's tenuous hold on tentative gains versus old homeostatic patterns?

7. How does a pause by the therapist help create a context for the entire flow of therapy, as well as communicating a perspective on recent involvements with family members?

8. Why was it important for the therapist to reframe the patient's labeling of herself as in a state of "collapse" to a "regaining her sense of self enough to reach out for help"? How is this evidence of her growing strength?

9. *When the patient is reminded of the larger picture of progress in the shared context of their work together, what do you notice about the patient's ability to reclaim her own strength and growing confidence?*

10. *Discuss how the conscious verbalization of shame can retrigger and reactivate old organizing schemas around coping. What role does the therapeutic relationship play in helping sustain the memory of therapeutic gains?*

THE CONNECTION BETWEEN SHAME AND TRAUMA

Judith Herman (1997) persuasively speaks to how trauma often leads to a fracturing and fragmentation of the self.

Traumatic reactions occur when action is of no avail. When neither resistance nor escape is possible, the human system of self-defense becomes overwhelmed and disorganized. . . . Traumatic symptoms have a tendency to become disconnected from their source and to take on a life of their own.

(p. 34)

Such disconnection expresses well the basis of dissociative process. Traumatic environments leave in their wake damaging side effects. Because the individual can neither resist nor escape, the person is hard pressed to give some explanation as to *why this happened.* Finding a reason *why* is often an attempt to help stabilize an overwhelmed and disorganized self.

It seems most young children are vulnerable to making meaning of why trauma happened by *blaming the self.* They make sense out of *why* by calling themselves defective. For example, if they were strong enough, this wouldn't have happened. If they were good enough, Mommy wouldn't be so mean. Thus, we see the pairing of trauma and shame.

The costly side effects of trauma and the attendant internalization of feelings of shame and worthlessness can be summarized as follows:

- Trauma interferes with the development of authenticity through insecure or disorganized primary attachments.
- Traumatized children develop a core belief that they are defective, evil, or unworthy, with attendant feelings of shame that in turn must be defended against.
- The effects of internalized trauma can be clinically measured by observing a number of critical characteristics:

  - Low self-esteem.
  - Inability to trust.
  - Relationship difficulties.
  - Somatic issues.
  - High sensitivity to misattunement that often triggers feelings of despair.

Individuals often attempt to protect themselves from the re-experience of trauma by avoiding areas of psychic vulnerability involving feelings of shame or worthlessness. The Four Quadrant Model creates a fluid picture of how traumatically induced defensive strategies come into play.

THE CONNECTION BETWEEN SHAME AND DESPAIR

Hovering alongside unmetabolized shame is the companion experience of despair. Shame and despair weave a complicated network of interactions in a patient's relational organizing schema. Like shame, despair is both an emotion and a belief system. While shame says, "This is who I am," despair says, "I'm helpless to do anything about it." Despair is the secret conviction that lurks beneath the surface of shame. When proactive efforts or certain degrees of risk-taking are required, despair says, "Why bother, nothing will change anyway."

From a dynamic perspective, compensatory strategies used to distance from feelings of shame and unworthiness eventually fail. As a result, feelings of despair emerge, often creating a psychic state of immobilization. A chronic pattern develops when available psychic energy over time begins to wear thin. This may occur when persistent disappointments mount or when present-day trauma activates a cascade of emotions associated with fear and dread. As systems become further and further taxed, dissociative mechanisms become amplified. This is evidenced by further constriction, withdrawal, or contempt for self or others. The culmination often results in a state of passive resignation, ranging from feelings of apathy to suicidal ideation.

From a neurophysiological perspective, despair results from intense fear over a prolonged time period. When fear of annihilation becomes so great and the neuro-circuitry systems become so overloaded, the body/psyche begins to shut down. In his research on the stress response circuitry in infants, Allan Schore

(1996) has found that children reflexively decrease emotional arousal as a means of preserving neural growth. Robert Neborsky (2003) makes a similar point when adults are faced with situations of severe danger or trauma. Again, often reflexively, a sense of emotional detachment takes over in acute situations of danger. The narrowing of affect enables the individual to prevent panic, which Neborsky identifies as an innate mechanism for self-preservation.

In clinical work, we see that among individuals wrestling with a specific situation of danger, those with healthy, secure childhood environments tend to recover with little permanent residual damage, generally within a specified time frame. Individuals with a childhood history of relational failure, abuse, or neglect, however, do not recover as quickly or as easily. For them, many traumas appear to open a sealed doorway of vulnerability that is both frightening and dysregulating.

In our next section, a written case example is offered, illustrating how a combination of insecure or traumatic childhood attachments coupled with present-day disappointments can trigger feelings of passive resignation. In a circular fashion, a resigned position functions in an attempt to shut down feelings of loss, disappointment, or despair. This shutting down further intensifies feelings of resignation and hopelessness.

Written Case Example: Depression and Profound Resignation

A patient with feelings of depression and characterological resignation combined with perfectionistic standards entered treatment but with some degree of ambivalence. He only agreed to do so when his wife threatened to leave him if he didn't seek help. The wife's concerns and frustrations centered on the patient's growing personalized immobilization and distancing from family and friends. This disengagement eventually involved a reduced capacity for self-care, including neglected hygiene, poor eating and sleeping habits, and disinterest in work.

Family history included a mother who displayed magical thinking around her son's "god-like" attributes, and who displayed growing signs of mania coupled with delusional thinking and paranoia. After the parents divorced when the patient was seven, he was left alone with his mother as she slowly deteriorated into further paranoia. The patient adopted the role of the loyal soldier, minimizing his mother's actions while trying to live up to her high hopes for his success. At age seventeen, however, just prior to the patient leaving home and entering college, his mother committed suicide.

This tragedy left the patient "not remembering or feeling much of anything after that." He failed to enroll in college, found part-time work, and eventually completed a four-year degree at a local college. However, he remained relatively isolated, making few friends until he met his wife, who was seven years his senior. The relationship appeared to be relatively happy until the patient had a severe car accident. The trauma left him in extreme pain, which required a protracted course of pain medication, and leg and hip surgery that resulted in an inability to walk without a severe limp. According to his wife, the patient never recovered from this episode, and the spiral of depression, self-hate, estrangement, and feelings of suicidal ideation intensified.

After two years in treatment, the patient showed increasing signs of trust in the therapeutic relationship, improved mood and productivity at work, as well as attention to the nurturing of his young son. However, his difficulty with self-image and his pursuit of outside interests continued.

Following a session where the patient had been confronted by various family members as well as his wife around his continued difficulty with self-care, the therapist asked him what he made of his seeming inability to follow-through on agreed-upon initiatives. The patient said, "I guess there's an element of self-punishment here."

The therapist responded by asking, "Is there anything else this might be saying to us?"

The patient's immediate response was, "Well, maybe it's just a way of saying screw it all. Maybe I just secretly believe, why bother? It's not going to amount to anything anyway. Sooner or later some other horrible disappointment is going to blindside me once again. Why bother?"

The therapist quietly asked, "I'm wondering if this belief, that efforts don't matter, might have something to do with your mother's suicide." The patient had a blank, puzzled look, stating he couldn't see the connection.

The therapist reflected that he sounded like someone who deep down was pretty defeated and hopeless, believing that any efforts he initiated wouldn't make any difference in the long run.

Genuinely puzzled, the patient replied that he couldn't see the connection to his mother's suicide. "The only feeling I was left with after that tragedy was being shocked and really sad for her."

Discussion Questions

1. *Explain the relationship between lack of self-care and underlying feelings of passive resignation or despair.*

2. *What role do you think the mother's marked over-idealization had on the patient's sense of self?*

3. *Discuss how you think all four quadrants can be simultaneously activated by the mother's suicide.*

4. *What role does shame play in keeping the patient immobilized?*

5. *How does the feeling of despair both activate deeper feelings of shame as well as maintain an old homeostatic balance?*

6. *What role does the patient's perfectionism play in maintaining the patient's old organizing schemas and in deepening his feelings of despair?*

THE CONNECTIONS BETWEEN SHAME, SELF-HATE, AND IDEALIZATION

The more one experiences the ravages of self-hate, the more one appreciates the immense role it plays in psychological disorders. It has been called a "cruel and merciless force" (Horney, 1950) that derives its power from its insidious interpenetration with every other aspect of the patient's distress. Self-hate has the power to compound and multiply on itself by pushing the person to potentially dangerous levels of self-contempt.

It is very difficult to talk about self-hate without at once talking about its intimate companion, shame. Each can intensify the other in a ruthless cycle of suffering: *I am ashamed of being such a pitiful person and hate myself for it.*

Insofar as the therapist can maintain some sense of optimism amidst these furies, the question arises as to where such a debilitating cycle gets its enormous power? The answer lies in the deeper understanding that we do *not* really despise ourselves because we are without assets, but because we have been driven by fears and anxieties to compulsive pursuits of unattainable and precarious idealizations.

Vulnerable to our pain, we have little control over these vicious cycles. Without help, we are essentially victims to our seemingly hope-creating but actually hope-denying idealized creations. But treatment becomes our evermore reliable ally. Evidence begins to mount that these cycles are ridden with conflicts and contradictions and that we have willy-nilly boxed ourselves into unattainable belief systems divorced from any attainable reality. With these slowly developing insights, authenticity begins to assert itself, and health is now fueling *itself* rather than being co-opted by negative forces.

Empathic immersion has proven to be our best posture in being able to monitor and access these sensitive issues. Disguised communications become more available to us moment-to-moment. As treatment unfolds, trust, hope, and optimism build not only in our patients but also in ourselves.

In the earlier case vignette about the patient whose mother committed suicide, we saw a relationship between shame and despair. Beyond that relationship, the vignette can further open our discussion to seeing the interconnection between high degrees of syntonic perfectionism highlighted in Quadrant One with now obvious manifestations of self-hate in Quadrant Four. Both dystonic shame and despair are involved in this relationship as well, but now the dynamics include highly syntonic elements. Here the vicious cycle of the patient's adherence to a belief in his mother's wish for his achievement of greatness and special status *also* connects to relational triggers of loyalty to the mother's personal needs for her son's perfectionism. The difficulty in giving up unrealizable standards is both an expression of remaining loyal to the mother's attachment to her son as well as being a continual reminder that no matter what he does in his life, it would never be enough to bring his mother back. Thus, despair, shame, and self-hate keep the patient locked in frozen immobility while he maintains a fierce loyalty to mother.

In the following two videos, we strive to highlight the subjective power of these conflicts and contradictions, and the therapist's simultaneous awareness of both the health and non-health in the patient's life. In the first case vignette, the patient has resolved considerable feelings of anger and low self-esteem by working through early childhood disappointments toward a withholding and very critical mother. However, his feelings around his father's alcoholism and physical abuse of his older brother have remained unresolved. The patient escaped the critical eye of his father's judgment and abuse by achieving high standards of success both academically and in his professional career. He escaped the physical trauma experienced by his older brother, but he maintains feelings of shameful guilt for not having spoken up to take a stand against the abuse directed at his brother.

Here we see the eruption of shame surface more directly. Yet, the shame was essentially silent until it could be broached in the treatment. Notice the level of dissociation around specific "shameful" behaviors that need to be accessed before they can be understood and accepted.

Please refer to the Routledge website, Video 7.2: Quadrant Four, Shame and Self-Hate.

Questions for Discussion

1. *What function does the patient's self-hate have early in this case scenario as he tries to recount the event at work?*

2. *How does this feeling of self-hate contribute to his dissociation about throwing his friend "under the bus"?*

3. *How does the therapist slow the patient down in the present moment to help him begin to recover from his dissociative "amnesia"?*

4. *Comment on how the patient is flooded with feelings of shame once the dissociation lifts.*

5. *How does the therapist help make connections to the patient's fear of his father's rage, the patient's resulting survival techniques, and his ability to apologize to his friend in the present moment?*

6. *Discuss how the patient's shaming of his friend is a dissociated enactment of his father's treatment of family members.*

7. *How does the therapist "normalize" the patient's actions when she points out their connection to terror, and how does she normalize the patient's learned survival response as well?*

---

8. How can a therapist deal with shame in treatment in a way that does not contribute to therapist burnout?

In our next video illustrating how shame sensitivity manifests itself, we offer an example of how over-idealization of one's therapeutic efforts can create feelings of self-recrimination and exhaustion when caretaking efforts fail. In this scenario, we find a patient who is also a therapist talking with her therapist about the pressure and sense of failure she feels when she is unable to help a patient with Crohn's disease. Notice how the therapist's empathy for her patient becomes confused with an over-identification with her patient's feelings of shame around the disease and her feelings of shame in not being able to alleviate the patient's overpowering shame over his disease.

This case illustration also exemplifies the contagious effect of shame on individuals with high degrees of shame sensitivity. However, the supervising therapist is able to use this discussion to facilitate a breakthrough in achieving a more realistic perspective on what is helpful. In doing so, we see developing signs of the patient's health and resilience breaking through.

Please refer to Routledge website, Video 7.3: Over-Helpfulness and Idealization.

Questions for Discussion

1. How does the therapist help his patient change her perspective around her over-determined measures of what she considers to be helpful?

2. Describe how the patient's measure of career success is connected to her relationship with her mother's early childhood demands.

3. How does the patient's loyalty to her mother's demands transfer into her idea of what it means to be a good therapist?

4. *What is the cost to the patient to maintain these loyalty standards?*

5. *What is the cost/risk of imposing this over-determined standard onto her clinical work?*

6. *When the patient says, "It bothers me so much," notice that the therapist asks for further clarification as to how/why this bothers her. Discuss how this entry-point "tracking comment" is helpful to further the dialogue, which begins to uncover the patient's own shame.*

7. *The therapist then shifts to the husband's reactions to the patient bringing her work home with her. He continues to ask questions that illuminate more detail about her husband's history and his capacity to be a caretaker.*

   a. *What do you think about this shift in focus?*

   b. *What might be the reasoning behind this line of inquiry at this particular moment?*

   c. *Would you have done something differently?*

8. *The therapist then shifts to the patient as caretaker in her own family of origin. The patient reveals more information about her mother and father's dynamic, specifically her role of caretaker of her mother when her father "shamed" her mother. Notice that the therapist now brings up shame more directly. By uncovering this family system dynamic, he is better able to connect current shame with past shame.*

a. *Discuss the timing of the therapist's first, second, third, and fourth references to shame.*

b. *Explain how connecting the patient's caretaking of her own mother's shame has given the supervising therapist greater leverage to explore her patient's feelings of "vicarious shame" with regard to feeling helpless in the face of her own patient's Crohn's disease.*

9. *The therapist then "normalizes" the patient's strong reaction of not being able to help, stating, "We all have these feelings at times." He then asks if the feelings sometimes are embarrassing. The patient becomes very hard on herself, at which point the therapist reminds her that she knows that she has been helpful to many people in the past. How do you assess the therapist's attempts to penetrate the patient's over-determined standards (which is an example of Quadrant One)?*

10. *Finally, the therapist then explores the ways in which the patient is hard on herself even when the situation can't be fixed. He wonders about whether she can still see herself as a good person, even in the face of not being able to "fix" something.*

a. *What do you make of the therapist's use of support and validation at this moment?*

b. *Describe any shift that occurred for the patient at that point.*

Our third case illustrates a three-part vignette that tracks a progression of insights, dreams, and reflections that are related to the patient's history of sexual abuse. By way of background, this is a 54-year-old man who grew up in a small Midwestern town where his family engaged in a religious cult that practiced ritualistic abuse. The patient remembers that he as well as his twin sisters were a part of this cult's practices. Neither sister is able to access any memory of early childhood abuse. (It should be noted that this series of successive vignettes are excerpts taken when the patient was four years into his treatment.)

Earlier flashbacks of actual physical abuse had vividly surfaced five years ago through a prior therapy. In that therapy, the patient was able to retrieve partial memories of ritualistic group sexual abuse. He also recalled that if he tried to resist, physical abuse and verbal threats occurred.

In the earlier parts of his current therapy, the patient focused on his over-determined efforts around performance as well as relational disappoint-ments and wishes to retaliate or withdraw. As the patient continued to make progress, further memories of sexual abuse continued to break through.

*Note: The following series of case vignettes is highly graphic. Some readers may find this uncomfortable or disturbing. Read at your own discretion.

Please refer to the Routledge website, Video 7.4: Traumatic Shame, Part One.

Patient:	I want to begin by sharing a memory fragment that came to me as I was listening to Rick Hansen's guided meditation. I stayed with the fragment, and when I did, more memories began to flood in. I have to warn you, it got pretty graphic.
Therapist:	Go on.
Patient:	(He then begins reading from his journal.) I had an image of being held down. Several guys were holding my arms and legs so I wouldn't resist. They began to sequentially rape me.
Therapist:	How old were you in this image?
Patient:	I was 4 and a half or 5 years old. Then I had the sense that there was a doctor who was there. He gave me some kind of shot, I think to either put me out or make me block the memory of what occurred. I also remember my mother slapping me on the face so I'd cooperate, and that man held a knife to my throat again. That's all I remember.
Therapist:	What happened after this memory surfaced?
Patient:	Well I didn't become unglued. I decided to listen to the guided meditation tape again, only this time I imagined taking the knife from the man and stabbing each one of them. It was enormously freeing. (Pause) But I was also uncomfortable because I was aware that these memories had triggered a subtle form of aggression in me. I couldn't shake the feeling. Two days later, I had a bad meditation. On some level, I was sensing that the earlier medita-tion and the graphic memories had broken the lid off of some-thing. That sense of relief and sense of freedom I initially felt

were replaced with a sense of uneasiness, like there were more hidden fragments that were about to emerge. So I began my regular meditation routine anyway yesterday morning. After a few moments, I saw an image of a dirty, soiled rag. I knew that this represented me—dirty and soiled by what had been done to me. I was reduced to a rag. This image was immediately followed by a memory flash of men leaving semen on my skin, and I felt them each inserting their penis into me. Then, the image shifted again, and I saw myself trying to wash the rag, first in a basin, then a stream, then in a waterfall. And then I saw the figure of Jesus joining me, taking the rag in his own hand, taking the rag that was now white and washing it in baptismal water. Then, I saw an image of that square rag turn into a diamond, and I saw the diamond rise up into the air and break up into a million pieces. I began breathing it in and it filled me with the light, with the light of *God.*

Note: After this dream session and our subsequent sessions, the patient was lighter and more spontaneously happy, resolving multiple relational difficulties. However, four months later, the patient again lapsed into a funk, describing vague feelings of depression and anxiety. We were able to trace the anxiety and depression to a growing realization that his childhood environment was "crazy." He admitted to me that both of his parents, due to their own damage, were highly destructive.

Very next session: Please refer to the Routledge website, Video 7.5: Traumatic Shame, Part Two.

The patient begins this session by reviewing our last session, reminding me that his greatest take-away was that he was able to clearly and freely verbalize that his early childhood environment was "crazy." Rather than equivocating or excusing his parents as he had in the past (where we see old forms of loyalty protecting the image of his parents as being more benign than they were), he had now come to the point where he was able to forcefully state that he knew at the core of his being that his environment had been crazy and abusive. He begins the content of this session with a dream that he had had the evening directly after our last session.

Dream: *I was walking into a church chapel and there is a man age 50 and a woman who reminded me of my mother. There was an altar somewhat obscuring my view of the man near the altar. The woman was carrying baking mixing bowls, big enough to hold a head. The bowls were brought forward. The man checks the size of the bowl to see if it was big enough for his head. There were instruments on the altar, and I then realized that they were preparing to be beheaded. I sensed a presence of another person (or force) that was going to be* *performing the beheading. It was as if these two people had committed horrible offenses, and a higher order of justice required their punishment by a beheading on the altar of the sanctuary.*

Then I woke up, unnerved and deeply troubled by the dream. In the morning I wrote questions for self-reflection. I never would want to sever a head from a body, yet, I had to ask myself, "Is this my deep-seated rage?" "Are the man and woman at the altar symbols of my parents, and my unconscious is showing me that I secretly harbor a wish to kill them?"

"Does the dream signify the shutting down of my more tender energy?" "Was I finally ending the 'life' of my parents' influence in my being, my memory?"

The intensity of the dream so closely following my last session with you didn't escape me.

Therapist:	Are you saying that the naming of the crazy environment as a child may have evoked the dream?
Patient:	Yes.
Therapist:	Whenever you make a statement that clarifies a truth that's been hidden around trauma, something generally will come up to confirm or reveal something more. It could be a missing part of the puzzle that we've yet to integrate, or it could be some sort of consolidation that your dream is reinforcing. Where might your thoughts go from here? What further associations do you have?
Patient:	Well, the first piece—why was it taking place in a quasi-chapel, which would normally be a place of healing and devotion versus such violence? The second piece—one man, one woman. They both seemed to be entering into this willingly. And the piece of the dream that was so repulsive—that someone would willingly subject themselves to having their head cut off is puzzling. (Long pause) Do they have to be beheaded to eliminate their presence?
Therapist:	Beheaded by whom?
Patient:	That's not clear. Something is presiding, but there is no face, no body.
Therapist:	So, what's the something?
Patient:	I don't know whether it's some priestly person.
Therapist:	But you said it didn't have a body. What else might it be?
Patient:	A judging spirit?
Therapist:	What was your sense about the presence? Was the spirit or presence malevolent or neutral?
Patient:	If I had to calibrate it, it was a spirit that was there to give a punishment for something deserved. But I don't understand why each character would willingly put themselves in that position. (Pause) Hm, a thought I just had—if I'm in the dream, if there are parts of

the dream that are me, am I getting rid of parts of my father and crazy parts of my mother?

Therapist: What's the significance of cutting off the head? Why that part?

Patient: My first (and only) EMDR experience was a flashback I had that revealed a knife at my throat. (Long pause) I don't know. I'm not coming up with anything. Why would you use bowls, to make it tidier when you get done?

Therapist: I'm afraid we're out of time. You know, John, I've been careful not to put forward my own interpretation of the dream just yet. Intuitively, my sense is to let you sit with this for a bit more time. It seems to be an important dream. Why don't you see what comes up during the week, what may come into your consciousness. Use your journaling to sit and free associate a bit—to see where this might take us.

Third session: Please refer to the Routledge website, Video 7.6: Traumatic Shame, Part Three.

Patient: Ok, I continued to work with my associations to the dream. First, on the righteous side, there was the action of punishment for treating children as if they don't matter. And that makes sense to me given my abuse. On the uncomfortable side, it's the extent of the anger that is symbolized in the dream that bothers me—as if a part of me *wants* to exact punishment for the injustice done to me. (Pause) Part of what has unfolded over the past week is "me identifying what belongs to me." For so long, I internalized the belief of being an object—because I was abused so brutally, I must not have been important. Also, something else is emerging at the same time—it has to do with being human and humanity as opposed to being objects—all of us, not just my situation, but so many people in the world treating each other as objects. Once I named the craziness in my family, it's as if the dream is allowing me to feel rage at the injustice everywhere. (Pause) You know, Molly (patient's wife) reminded me of the beginning of my conscious awareness of my anger toward my mother—it was something that happened in the late 1980s. We were married, and our kids were young. We had pictures of the family everywhere, but I didn't have any pictures of my mother anywhere, except for this small, little picture of her in a frame. I don't know what made me do this. It was before any of the breakthrough memories started to happen, but I remember going out back and taking the picture of my mother with me. I sat on the ground and took it out of the frame, and then I started stabbing it into little pieces, over and over again, until there was nothing left but little shreds of paper. Then, I waded it up in a ball and set it on fire. Years later, after the first memory of the knife at my throat, I remember going back to the old farmhouse where the abuse happened. I remember taking a knife with me and throwing it into the ground and leaving it there—sort of like saying, "Never again." After that, I went to the cemetery where my mother was buried, and I spit on her grave. (Pause) I've never told anyone about this except my wife.

Therapist: How does it feel telling me this now? Do you feel any sense of embarrassment or shame?

Patient: No, it's just a bit startling and uncomfortable. I don't think of myself as a violent person. But given the dream, I can't help but think that these earlier events are connected somehow. And now, since we've been working together for so long, I want to share it with someone, someone I trust. I trust you will help me make sense out of it.

Therapist: You said earlier that for so long you had internalized the belief that you deserved to be treated as an object. It is interesting that the moment you named the craziness as something outside of yourself, something you didn't have to feel ashamed about or responsible for in some way, that you were ready to get rid of that internalized belief. I'm wondering if the rage was a way for you to discharge and discard that old belief and all that attends it. Years ago, you demonstrated the rage physically through stabbing the picture and spitting on the grave, and it seemed to scare you a bit. Now that we've been uncovering these memories, things seem to be shifting. The dream allowed you to bring into consciousness the wish to destroy that which almost destroyed you.

Patient: But, I don't want to resort to violence and retaliation. That makes me no better than they were.

Therapist: But, isn't that part of your humanness too? Survival? The wish to survive when our lives are being threatened is also a part of our humanness and our vulnerability.

Patient: (Patient begins sobbing) You're right. They would have killed me if I had resisted. They took away my innocence. Of course there is a part of me that wished they were dead.

Therapist: You have a right to this wish. But, I want to remind you, that in the dream, you weren't the one who acted on the wish, someone else was there to enforce justice. Somewhere you must have developed the wish or belief that you didn't have to take this burden upon yourself. In real life, you never fell over the edge; you never really resorted to violence or even self-destructive acts when you were younger. Many people with your history do fall into this pattern. The extent of the abuse you suffered could have destroyed you, *almost* destroyed you. But it didn't. You held the boundary,

Patient: even when your mother and the others violated the boundary, you found a way not to.

Patient: Yeah, a human standard was violated. Standards are violated everywhere, aren't they? And the lack of compassion in so many people is enraging. You're helping me see that rage is a normal feeling, but it's a wish that I'm not necessarily acting on. The wish is both for survival and for justice. (Pause) The delicacy in all of what you just summed up is that it *almost* destroyed me. But it didn't. Somehow, I managed to keep my humanity.

Therapist: And it's the *almost* that allowed more of your real self to emerge, to gain access to your vulnerability in ways that continue to soften you. You told me about crying during the documentary of the prison choir, and the innocence of the children at the Christmas church service. And then, when you were in your car, you told me about being in touch with your vulnerability and your openness in such a pure way. The rage you have felt over the years, and the rage you allowed yourself to access in your dream, was discharged in a controlled, understandably intense enough way that it worked. And it has to be intense enough to get rid of the introject—what you had internalized.

Patient: Yes, you called it not falling over the edge. It's a boundary. In my life, there has always been a hard stop—not acting out the destruction. And that hard stop is between good and evil. When you've been abused, the world becomes very absolute—right, wrong, there's no grey. And yet there is a wish that I have that is in the grey zone. The grey zone is expressing what is legitimate but without injury to others. It has to do with finding a way to express the intensity but without the negative consequences to myself or without harming others.

Questions for Discussion

1. *In the first vignette segment, the patient's meditation helped him access a memory fragment where he referenced himself as a soiled rag. How could you formulate an explanation around his attempts at washing the rag as:*

   a. *A wish to be free from shame and contamination?*

b. A sign of health and personal agency?

2. How would you work with the patient's next visualization where he saw the figure of Jesus taking the rag and making it pure, followed by the image of the rag turning into a diamond that broke up into pieces and filled him with the light of God?

3. In the next segment, the patient was able to report that he experienced a powerful and liberating "take-away" when he was able to verbally declare that his "early childhood was crazy."

   a. How might this reflect a shift away from old loyalty patterns?

   b. How does the externalization of "craziness," now not owned by him anymore, help to ameliorate feelings of internalized shame?

4. How does the subsequent dream support further signs of this loyalty shift?

   a. Why do you think that there was a third person in the dream administering justice?

   b. How might you work with the patient around his own feelings of anger, aggression, and the wish for justice?

5. When the patient makes the connection between the dream and his earlier assertion around his parents being "crazy," how does the therapist help to reinforce this connection?

6. In the third session, we see that the patient is able to work with his own feelings of aggression more directly.

   a. What would you say about the patient's level of trust with the therapist allowing him to admit to wishes and actions around feelings of rage and aggression?

   b. How is this a further sign of health?

   c. How might this also free up the patient around secondary feelings of shame around his wish for retaliation?

7. How is the therapist able to help the patient neutralize and normalize these feelings?

8. Together the patient and the therapist are able to name his ability to make a "hard stop," a boundary where the reenactment of the aggression does not cross a line into destructiveness.

   a. How does this further shift the sense of relational loyalty as well as personal self-worth for the patient?

   b. How are the feelings of shame and unworthiness further lifted off of the patient's shoulders?

   c. Explain how this in turn lessens over-determined efforts and the need to overcompensate by "proving" himself.

THE CONNECTION BETWEEN SHAME AND ADDICTION

The field of addiction has evolved to the point where both 12-step programs (AA, NA, GA, SA, OA, and others) and addiction practitioners agree that shame is intricately involved at many levels in the development of addiction. The relationship is both reciprocal and mutually reinforcing. Substances can make shame-prone people feel greater or less shame about themselves while addiction always compounds the shame. Potter-Effron (2011) has called this a "shame-addiction spiral" (p. 221) and describes how "embarrassing incidents become shaming and then humiliating" (p. 222), leading to an ever-spiraling cycle.

Therapists are mindful that shame is often a painfully hidden emotion within patients, their families, and the society at large. This puts a higher burden on the therapist to maintain trust in a caring supportive relationship. Cognitive therapy can be helpful in countering blanket accusations of self-blame by patients caught in the shame-addiction spiral (Dearing and Tangney, 2011). However, locating and working through the underlying feelings of inadequacy, emptiness, or isolation that drive the addiction spiral are more completely addressed with a dynamic understanding of the compensatory efforts that are set up in the service of avoiding shame.

Perhaps the most difficult situation a therapist can face with addicted patients is the defensive posture of exhibitionism (Potter-Effron, 2011). Both shamelessness and exhibitionism are defenses against shame. Shame-prone addicted individuals are in Potter-Effron's words, "highly aggressive in response to a perceived attack, developing a shame-rage pattern that can be highly dangerous to anyone who intentionally or unintentionally triggers their internal shame alarm" (p. 227). Within the context of shame dynamics, the phenomenon of exhibitionism is intimately connected to the aspiration of becoming pridefully invulnerable.

Despite these potentially dangerous trends, there is a reason why addicts attend 12-step programs through the world in ever-increasing numbers. The ability to reach the point where one can say *I am helpless* can be a huge turning point in whatever type of psychotherapy is involved with these patients.

SUMMARY

Shame is inextricably involved in dissociation, disavowal, disconnection, splitting, and alienation. As such we have placed it squarely in the epicenter of our Four Quadrant process grid. It fuels and systemically ties together all four quadrants. No quadrant stands alone. As a process grid, any perturbation in any quadrant immediately resonates with the other quadrants such that all quadrants are quintessentially involved. Thus, *all* the quadrants operate to form a unifying mechanism to defend against shame and shame derivatives.

Shame is born out of failures in primary relationships, but the failures do not remain static. Shame affects all relationships, certainly including the relationship between patient and therapist. There is an almost unique contagious quality to shame whereby each level of struggle, disappointment, or experienced alienation creates yet more shame (either visible or hidden) that then creates further debilitating cycles of conflict or withdrawal. As we have emphasized, shame begets shame. Short of therapeutic intervention, there is frequently little respite from these compulsively driven mechanisms.

Lest this cycle seem hopeless to you, be aware that major advances have been made in the treatment of shame in the last few decades, including a much deeper understanding of trauma and the entire dissociative spectrum. We might say that trauma has educated us on the understanding of shame and hence on more effective therapeutic interventions.

As with so much else in psychotherapy, access to shame becomes more possible the more we can stay in the *present* (Danielian and Gianotti, 2012). In a negative paradox, it has the power to dramatically increase the contagion effect, the more access we can have to it in the experiential moment. It is certainly a "hot" emotion. Once we pick it up, the impulse is to toss it as quickly as we can. Both professionally as well as culturally, this might explain why it is so difficult to acknowledge the powerful grip shame exerts on individual and collective consciousness.

The connection between shame and society has gone largely unaddressed. Yet shame has fueled our increasing preoccupation with appearance, our fear and disgust around the normal aging process, our admiration of those who are rich and famous regardless of their deeds or character, and our seeming addiction to acquiring greater and greater degrees of material wealth. The fear of being "less than" allows for the turning of a blind eye to social issues around justice and fairness, thus creating a more segregated and polarized populace. Rudeness and manipulation replace kindness, "getting what's mine" becomes more important that seeing the interconnection between all human beings. These cultural trends around what has become increasingly tolerated (and even normalized) are largely based on the avoidance of naming the power that shame holds over the psyche.

8

Introduction to Transference

Transference thus provides a means for exploring the way in which a person sees life; it provides the material that makes up our "inner representational world." The other person's inner representational world is what therapists need to enter if they are to understand those with whom they work. The other person's inner world is their "psychic reality," their belief that the world is made "as if" it were how they see it.

—Robert W. Rentoul (2010, p. 78)

[T]he interplay between transference and countertransference [is] an intersubjective process reflecting the mutual interaction between the differently organized subjective worlds of patient and analyst . . .

—Stolorow (2013, p. 384)

Transference is probably the most misunderstood and underutilized tool of our trade. Many graduate training programs no longer give credence to the existence of transference, much less teach students how to work with transference dynamics. As such, many practicing clinicians feel ill-equipped to enter into this arena of the therapeutic relationship. Without adequate training, therapist reactions to transference frequently bring up a myriad of feelings ranging from avoidance to confusion to dread.

Misunderstandings about the benefits of working with transference may in large measure stem from a reaction against early analytic postures that were informed and guided by a "one-person" approach to the therapeutic relationship. This theoretical viewpoint held that the analyst was an objective, neutral observer, a blank screen on which the patient would eventually project feelings and assumptions from the past. Any negative reaction on the part of the patient then became *labeled* as resistance, manifesting as a "negative transference."

As we have shifted our posture toward more relational frameworks, a "two-person," intersubjective approach currently informs our understanding of transferential dynamics. This shift in perspective requires the therapist to continually assess and monitor whether a patient's charged feelings, either positive or negative, stem from missed cues on the therapist's part or whether the patient's response is being triggered by historically rooted emotions and assumptions.

From a relational perspective, the shift toward a two-person approach to transference has profound implications on the therapeutic process. Increased awareness around the impact of the therapist's own style, biases, and blind spots help us equalize the dynamic between the patient and therapist, hopefully reducing the potential for shame and a perceived power imbalance. That being said, a relationally based orientation to working with transference requires a broadening of skill sets. No longer is an exclusive reliance on interpretation enough.

Even though many theoretical frameworks have adjusted, and practicing therapists have done their due diligence attempting to recover from the unfortunate misuse of analytic power, a few schools of thought seem to have made an *over-correction* that threatens to "throw the baby out with the bathwater." Here the baby is the productive dynamic of transference unfolding naturally in the service of healing and growth. Regardless of a clinician's theoretical paradigm and training, if we remain open to understanding the dynamic of transference in a neutral or curious way, transference can at the very least be conceptualized as the patient's expanded experience of the therapist.

A second misunderstanding or missed opportunity around working with transference has to do with how contemporary training programs approach the subject matter. Most training focuses on the extremes of the affective continuum regarding transference. Examples used for training illustrations either present a highly over-idealized positive transference or a highly charged negative transference. Although these extremes of affective responses do occur, especially with individuals with "borderline presentations," milder or more hidden dimensions of transference occur throughout the therapeutic process. As Paul Wachtel (1993) states,

[T]he either-or approach in which establishing the contribution of the patient's past and of his personality structure seems to require that the transference reaction be seen as having nothing to do with the reality of the ongoing transaction with the therapist . . . ongoing transactions [are involved] in all aspects of the patient's functioning, between internal processes and previous history on the one hand, and the events and persons encountered at the moment on the other.

(p. 55)

AN OVERVIEW OF TRANSFERENCE FROM A RELATIONAL PERSPECTIVE

Transference emerges out of the subjective relational stew that is part of the therapeutic process. Its emergence is non-linear; that is, we see parts of the real self intertwine with defensively driven patterns of the character solution. As one becomes more accustomed to the relational stew, it becomes easier to tease apart and palpate the therapeutic dialogue in a way that enables hidden transferential material to emerge more consciously.

When working with transference, one begins by asking the question, "What is it that is being *transferred* in the transference dynamic?" To answer this question, we advise the therapist to explore areas within the patient's presentation where shame, fear, or dissociated aspects of the self threaten to disrupt the existing homeostasis of the character structure. Ironically, gains in the treatment eventually begin to threaten the old homeostatic balance of the character solution, leading to unconscious or dissociated transferential testing of the therapeutic bond.

Initially, the manifestation of transferential material occurs through an enactment, either directly with the therapist, or through reported "derivative" recounting of enactments in the outside world. *Transferential enactments are actually one of the ways that the historical past is revealed to us within the treatment.* The therapeutic opportunity then lies in connecting the unfolding enactment in the experiential present to dissociated memories, fears, and expectations from the historical past. Eventually, as the therapist palpates the dialogic exchange, transference feelings, wishes, and longings begin to be articulated.

Working with transference means working in the subjective *present* because, without doubt, this is where the therapeutic dialogue becomes personal. Transference is *how* we gain direct access to the early organizing schemas of childhood, as we become more acutely aware of where and how the authentic self was derailed through failures in early attunement. It is a cumulative affair that can become prominent at any time but more typically as the patient's investment in the treatment increases, and the character structure becomes more tangible to both patient and therapist.

However, transference is not an exact replication of the past, because the relationship between the patient and the therapist is one that is constantly evolving (Cooper, 1987). As a more secure attachment builds between the therapist and patient, trust in the solidity of the relationship allows the patient to begin to reveal unconscious or dissociated transferential relational fears and expectations of others.

Over time, through repeated exchanges with the therapist, the patient's enactment begins to incorporate the live interaction between the patient and therapist in the living present. In that regard, there is no such thing as an enactment that is purely a repetition of the past. It is ever evolving and contextually triggered, and surprisingly, the dynamic becomes more consciously accessible to both therapist and patient through the nuances of the evolving relationship. Why? It is because therapist and patient are now meeting in the systemic moment, and a more open-ended dialogue can occur. Understanding now becomes a matter of the intersubjective present gradually enlarging to encompass the past.

But the real self is also unfolding and warrants careful attention. Taking the risk to reveal more of the real self requires trust in the therapeutic bond as well. Thus, in a "side-by-side" fashion, we see transferential material building on the real self as the real self gains strength and courage to emerge within the context of the therapeutic relationship. As the therapist is able to process and work through transferential enactments with the patient, the patient begins to feel more understood. When the therapist responds with thoughtful, careful holding, the patient's fears of retaliation or abandonment by the therapist begin to be released. Thus, the emergence of the real self can step forward even further.

From a positive, optimistic perspective, transference can be viewed as the highest state of intensity and "aliveness" the patient is showing us. Aliveness is an opportunity for health and integration to emerge. The more aliveness in the transference, the more internal resilience makes itself manifest. Herein lies the opportunity to use the therapeutic relationship in the service of healing and growth.

Our posture in this text is that transference, when understood as an enactment, is one of the most powerful leverage points at our disposal. With a present-focused relational framework, transference can be understood as *interpersonalizing* the patient's unconscious organizing schemas, bringing these schemas "alive" interpersonally and interactively through the therapeutic relationship. Based on this understanding, transference becomes a live here-and-now enactment of what lies at the heart of the patient's characterological structure.

Some readers may have wondered why we have not included repetition compulsion in our discussion thus far of transference. Historically, repetition compulsion had been a mainstay in traditional psychoanalysis; but with the field moving toward a systemic understanding of moment-to-moment tracking, the concept has lost its grounding. Both parts of the term "repetition compulsion" have been found to be too static and linear in scope. We now know, for example, that repetition is never actually repetition because it's never just in the past. A similar limitation applies to the term compulsion. A compulsion is never something just from the past but something constantly evolving in the present moment in dynamic ways. Efforts are now being made to "update" repetition compulsion to be seen as an enactment where the patient is experienced as most alive and hence most likely to be able to grow in strategic ways within the enactment. Since updated transference is a live enactment, it can now be seen constructively as a leading edge of growth. With these conceptual changes, the past becomes absorbed into the present, and the duality between past and present begins to disappear.

TRANSFERENCE AND THE FOUR QUADRANT MODEL

When we apply the Four Quadrant Model to transference, we are able to access feelings of shame most poignantly through palpating transferential material. From the vantage point of the Four Quadrant Model, transference can be viewed as a barometer of the characterological status of the patient at any given moment in the treatment.

Thus, working with transference is one of the ways that the Four Quadrant Model becomes operationalized. While the visual grid creates a snapshot of the still dissociated organizing schemas and their relational manifestations, it also importantly becomes an *active roadmap* as the therapist anticipates ways in which each of the quadrants plays its dynamic role in the transferential enactments. Put differently, enactments activate all four quadrants simultaneously and in real time.

To cite one possible example, if a patient comes in with complaints about relational disappointments in the outside world, eventually, those disappointments will be enacted within the therapeutic dynamic. We witness the unresolved longings contained in Quadrant Three become "live" within the transferential exchange. These disappointed longings activate issues across the entire process grid, and in particular, they mobilize often difficult negative transferential material from Quadrant Four.

As a process grid, the Four Quadrant Model is well suited as a guide for making interventions. One such intervention is the subtle palpating of incipient transferential material. The goal is to build enough "therapeutic muscle" for the patient to be able to deal with the eventual mobilization of more frankly negative transferential responses. We might define this "muscle" as the ability to use the therapeutic alliance to deal with formerly dissociated painful material.

As shameful feelings and wishes become metabolized and neutralized, we can begin to feel the exciting positive growth inherent in the process. Our reliable ally throughout this often tumultuous stage is the patient's growing sense of freedom of expression. This is how negative transference, from its protective cocoon, becomes reframed as the emergence of the authentic self.

At its core, the therapeutic position we offer is the suggestion for the therapist to "hold" a patient's negative transference by imagining that whatever a patient says or does cannot reduce the therapist's innate humanity. This means that the therapeutic holding response that is involved is one that is without retaliation, impatience, judgment, fear, or avoidance.

However, we are all human. We may or may not be able to "hold" a neutral stance in more extreme situations depending on our own vulnerabilities and past experience. We have found that working with more difficult or extreme cases of negative transference is universally challenging. By way of encouragement, even the most seasoned therapists may find difficulty maintaining the equilibrium to work through these challenging moments in the treatment. This is where face-to-face supervision is most useful and recommended.

ENHANCING SKILLS IN PALPATING NEGATIVE TRANSFERENCE

The ability to access any transferential feeling rests on the therapist's invitation to talk about the *experience* of therapy in an ongoing way. Asking questions that invite the patient to reflect on the therapy process and reflect on the treatment relationship is a form of *permission-giving* that opens a doorway to working with transference. We begin this section on palpating negative transference with a short video clip illustrating examples of how to ask general, non-threatening questions that give the patient permission to reflect on this important relational dimension of therapy.

Please refer to the Routledge website, Video 8.1: Palpating the Transference.

In this short supervision video, the reader will see that learning how to recognize and then "palpate" early signs of negative transference requires therapeutic attention around intrapsychic as well as relational dimensions of the psyche. Developing the skill of palpating the transference requires the therapist to cultivate a "listening ear" for off-handed comments that telegraph idealized wishes as well as devaluing comments. An example of an over-idealizing comment that a patient may make to the therapist is, "You would never do that to me. You're far too professional." Listening for signs of negative transference would require the therapist to focus on statements that telegraph how the patient reacts to disappointments, such as, "I guess all people are alike. You can never count on anyone to do a good job anymore."

Further inquiry into these off-handed comments is how one begins to palpate the transference. It is a matter of exploring what is beneath the tip of the iceberg. As we discussed in Chapter 5, this is where the technique of using language as an *entry point* can be applied to transferential exploration. For example, a therapist might palpate the over-idealizing comment by wondering, "What do you think would happen if you experienced me making a mistake, misunderstanding something you were trying to explain to me?" An example of how the therapist could palpate early signs of negative transference would be to ask, "Do you sometimes wonder if you can really count on me to do a good enough job in here?"

By asking these questions appropriately in the treatment, the therapist begins to set the stage for more in-depth exploration of the patient's automatic reactions and assumptions. This is a way of slowing the process down in the service of holding, containing, and modifying transferential reactions as they occur moment-to-moment. We have also found that applying these skills can help the therapist move into working with transference with more confidence and ease. Keeping watch for the emergence of both the over-idealized posture as well as the devaluing posture that occurs around any disappointment affords the therapist a clearer picture of the character solution along the *entire* spectrum from Quadrant One to Quadrant Four.

That being said, as the treatment progresses, manifestations of more charged expressions of transference will begin to surface when activated feelings around "loyal waiting" contained within Quadrant Three begin to be directed toward the therapist. Generally it takes some time for the longings of loyally waiting for rescue to actually *transfer* from relationships in the outside world to the therapist in the room. At some point in the treatment, formerly hidden magical wishes for the therapist to meet the patient's rescue needs without disappointment or shame now come into full view. This can occur when:

- The patient eventually loses patience with waiting for needs to be met without the patient directly asking.
- The patient experiences a disappointment in the therapist.
- The patient consciously experiences feelings of shame in the therapist's presence, either around the exposure of vulnerability or feeling "too needy" in the therapist's presence.

With patients who have more of a trauma history, the creation of a sturdy therapeutic holding environment is even more critical, as transference reactions can be triggered more easily. Even support can evoke fears around vulnerability, safety, and exposure of need. There may be conflicting desires to protect the therapist from patients' shame, rage, or defectiveness versus the need to unburden oneself and cut through one's sense of isolation.

In particular, loyalty struggles can manifest when the therapist has created a safe-enough holding environment that challenges the patient's old dictates of parental loyalty. In this situation, even slight ruptures in trust with a therapist can become a reenactment of a trauma, exposing the patient's fear of shameful neediness.

Another potential complication is that the presence of "therapeutic silence" may inadvertently stimulate feelings of pressure within the patient, wherein the patient may divulge secrets and hidden material prematurely. This may then evoke further feelings of shameful overexposure, since many patients with high degrees of shame sensitivity lack a consistent ability to manage their own affect-regulation. Thus, the therapist and the patient may experience a reactive relational struggle, where the patient *transferentially* believes that he or she must divulge material in an attempt to give the therapist what he or she wants. In turn, if the patient feels "coerced" into making disclosures prematurely, the safety and strength of the therapeutic alliance may experience a setback.

With more dysregulated or traumatized patients, boundaries become porous and can begin to collapse. This is certainly true of patients with borderline dynamics. The shakier boundaries become, the more the patient can experience the therapist as an adversary or potential abuser.

None of this means that the patient cannot make progress. If the therapist can empathically connect with this level of fearful negativity without retaliation, withdrawal, or hidden abuse, the patient can eventually appraise the therapist in less all-or-nothing terms. In particular, the patient will begin to be able to "touch" his "secret shame" that his abuse was not ever due to being defective or unworthy. The position of the therapist involves bearing therapeutic "witness" in a clinical setting. The treatment of patients with borderline dynamics is inevitably long-term, but the treatment courage involved in the growth process for both patient and therapist can be its own earned reward.

For training purposes in this chapter, we will focus on how positive and negative transferences commonly unfold in the course of treatment. However, additional relationship issues can affect the outcome of therapy as well. Persistent iatrogenic lapses (blind spots) by the therapist will likely affect outcome. If the therapist is prone to being "seduced" by flattering idealizations or basks in the positive transference of the patient, the treatment can easily be short-circuited. Another example of an iatrogenic lapse might be when an aggressive, anger-prone individual enters into treatment. If the therapist experiences discomfort and emotionally withdraws, the patient is likely to experience a lack of steady holding to help work through negatively charged patterns to a more effective resolution. (See Danielian and Gianotti, 2012, Chapter 8, for further examples).

CLINICAL APPLICATION OF THEORETICAL MATERIAL

The following section will offer three different examples of transferential statements delivered by a patient, followed by potential responses from the therapist. In each example, we will discuss the possible inroads that can be made with each statement.

Example 1. A patient with a history of early childhood sexual abuse coupled with a cold and withholding parental environment came into treatment due to relationship difficulties with an abusive boyfriend. The boyfriend's abuse was verbally directed at the patient's young children, and often sexually abusive behavior (forced) was directed at the patient. Although the patient tried numerous times to end the relationship with the help of the therapist, she continued to backslide into letting the boyfriend return. Upon entering the session, the patient says to the therapist:

Patient: **"This is the first time I *wasn't* looking forward to coming in to talk to you. I was afraid you would get angry with me because I let Joe come back into the apartment to stay with me. I hated myself afterwards."**

Therapeutic Response Options. *Here are Three Possible Options of What a Therapist Might Say in Response*

1. You mentioned that you weren't looking forward to coming in today. Were you afraid of coming in?

---

2. You hated yourself after you let Joe come back. Did you think I would judge you in a similar fashion?

3. Are you worried that I wouldn't understand why it is so difficult for you to set a limit with Joe?

Discussion and Analysis

In the first response, the therapist connects the patient's admission that she wasn't looking forward to coming to the session with the possibility of being afraid of the therapist's reaction. This statement creates an opening that would allow the patient to talk about either:

- The patient's secret wish to please the therapist.
- The patient's fear that if she doesn't "behave" in a manner that follows through consistently, she will disappoint the therapist.

In the second response, the therapist is inviting inquiry into Quadrant Four material as it might connect to Quadrant Three. Here the patient admits to self-hate, and the therapist opens a doorway of exploration into:

- Whether the patient expects others to treat her in a similar negative, punishing fashion.
- How performance is connected to self-loathing or possible retaliation on the part of "the other."

In the third response, the therapist is directing the patient's attention to issues of attunement and misattunement. In this case, the patient may be worried about:

- A break in the therapeutic alliance.
- Whether the therapist is really able to understand the pain involved in her own struggles around setting limits.

Example 2. A patient, who grew up in a family with a highly successful though distant father and a mother who always compared him to his older brother, comes into therapy because his wife has threatened to leave him. This patient prides himself on his business success, and he openly verbalizes contempt for people who are weak and needy. He is mystified and also angry that his wife suddenly announced that she wasn't happy, even though he had afforded her every luxury.

Patient: **"I always thought I knew my wife. This really surprised me and shook me up. I'm not the type of person who would come in here and complain about my wife."**

Therapeutic Response Options. *Here are Three Possible Options of What a Therapist Might Say in Response*

1. If we talk about your reaction to what your wife said about being unhappy, does that sound to you like it's complaining?

2. Is there something about the way she broke this news to you that is bothering you as well?

3. Can you tell me what it feels like talking with me about being shaken up by this news?

Discussion and Analysis

In the first response, the therapist is trying to explore the patient's thoughts and internalized standards around:

- Whether *any* emotional reaction is a sign of complaining, and, therefore, unnecessary.
- Whether his wife's unhappiness is a complaint against him, and therefore also unnecessary or a sign of betrayal of his standards.

- Whether there is more anger directed toward his wife that is being kept under wraps by labeling himself as complaining.

In the second response, the therapist is attempting to inquire about how the patient is feeling being caught off guard. For example:

- Is he more shaken up by his wife's unhappiness or his being caught off guard?
- Is he experiencing a sense of failure about not being able to anticipate every situation?

In the third response, the therapist is opening a pathway for the patient to share his fears about his vulnerability. By asking this question directly, the therapist can assess:

- The level of the patient's self-protection against shame and vulnerability.
- His ability to tolerate talking about feelings in the present moment more directly.

Example 3. A patient in his early thirties comes into therapy because he has had repeated difficulty forming long-lasting relationships. He will either pick detached, unavailable women, or he will pick women who become "too needy" and then looks for indications of a commitment, at which point the patient ends the relationship. After six months in therapy, he asks:

Patient: **"I've been going through a few psych books lately. You remember that I mentioned that I minored in psychology in my undergraduate studies. Well, I was reading in one of those books that eventually patients begin to feel like they're falling in love with their therapist. So doc, what do you think of that theory?"**

Therapeutic Response Options. *Here are Three Possible Options of What a Therapist Might Say in Response*

1. Is there any particular reason that you're wondering about that theory at this time?

> *2. You mean romantic feelings? Actually, that could get in the way of being helped in psychotherapy. What were you wondering about when you read that?*
>
> *3. It is true that therapy can feel like an intimate experience. That's because there aren't many situations where a person reveals so much of what is inside to another person. Does that sharing sometimes feel confusing to you?*

Discussion and Analysis

In the first response, the therapist asks why he might be wondering about the "theory" of falling in love with their therapist *at this time.*

The comment *at this time* directs the patient toward the present moment, reframing the conversation away from an intellectualized dialogue about theories in textbooks. By asking a more open-ended question about "why now," the therapist tries to gently probe into a possible transferential issue. The open-ended comment is designed to allow the patient to reveal as much as he is comfortable with doing at this time. When working with transferential comments in the early phases of treatment, it is better to touch lightly on the topic. One way to do that is by simply keeping the focus in the room on the present.

In the second response, the therapist comes forth with a question and statement, first asking a clarifying question that "names" the question of falling in love as romantic feelings, and then declaring that this could get in the way of being psychotherapeutically helpful.

In this instance, the therapist's comment may run the risk of shutting down transferential exploration. Still, the therapist's comment may have a supportive effect. For example, if the patient is feeling confused or flooded by his feelings on what he is reading, the therapist can create a boundary of safety for the patient. Conversely, if the patient is being provocative and challenging, the comment may act as a form of emotional containment.

In the third response, the therapist's comment is meant to have a psycho-educational impact.

It is meant to soothe the patient by noting the difference between self-disclosure inherent in the treatment dialogue and how infrequently this is encountered in the outside world. Note that the therapist then purposefully directs the patient to the possibility of confusing treatment and non-treatment situations, allowing for further information and affective material to reveal itself. Also note that the therapist is suggesting the possibility that sharing can be a positive experience, leading to deeper feelings about oneself and others.

Finally, the response is an example of forecasting—where the therapist introduces the idea that intimacy can exist *without* boundary violations. Our ultimate task here is to shore up boundaries while allowing for the real possibility that intimacy in the future can become less and less frightening.

VIDEO CASE VIGNETTES

In the previous section, we provided examples of one-line responses to potential transferential statements. Each question held different possibilities of what would be revealed next, thus encouraging further insight around the construction of each patient's particular character solution. This is how the Four Quadrant Model can be of service in delving more deeply into hidden material in the service of eventually creating a more secure attachment.

In this next section, we will examine more detailed transference exchanges via four videos. These videos illustrate how to work with transference from a relational and systemic posture. In each of the examples, we hope to demonstrate how moving carefully and systemically into the transference can make our therapeutic work more effective and considerably less daunting as well.

In the four videos provided below, please notice the times when the therapist moved more directly into the transference and times when transferential comments were handled more discreetly. This is due to issues of timing, readiness of the patient, context, and whether the treatment was in the early, middle, or later stages of therapy. Transferential work builds and increases in intensity as the therapeutic relationship evolves.

When transference material organically surfaces later in the treatment, we have an opportune moment to revisit earlier conflictual material associated with insecure attachment figures. However, if intense transferential material surfaces early on in the therapy (hopefully not iatrogenically derived), the characterological issues call for emotional containment and work around affect-regulation.

This first video on transference will give you an introduction of one supervisee's thoughts, illustrating how her growing comfort with using the Four Quadrant Model helped her "hear" when the emergence of transferential material began to surface. By listening for entry-point words and phrases that enabled her to move into transferentially based questions more naturally, the supervisee became increasingly comfortable with viewing transference as part of an organic unfolding of the therapeutic process.

Please refer to the Routledge website, Video: 8.1: Palpating the Transference.

In this brief supervision exchange, Jack and Patricia introduce the concept of palpating the transference. This gradual introduction into inviting transferential communication can be initiated by asking seemingly innocent questions that simply direct the patient to comment or reflect upon their experience in the room with the therapist at any given moment.

In the following video, we see a young woman with an over-idealizing transference. She has been in treatment for approximately two months. At the opening of this session, the patient makes a tentative transferential comment about feeling safe—"like if I'm heading for the shoals, you'll keep me safe. I suppose all of your patients tell you that." Then the patient immediately shifts to talking about her father. Notice how the therapist uses the initial inquiry process to get more contextual information about the family system, and the patient's sense of guilt and over-responsibility, choosing not to focus on her transferential statement at this time.

Please refer to the Routledge Website, Video: 8.2: Over-idealized Transference, Part 1.

Questions for Discussion

1. Why do you think the therapist initially bypassed the transferential statement, addressing instead the family's reaction to the father and how the entire family system responded to the father's critical nature?

2. What might have been the possible risks of directly addressing the transference this early in the relationship?

3. What impact does the therapist's comment have on the patient—where he distinguishes between the patient being responsible based on who she is versus being responsible because she was forced to be?

4. The patient's response begins to reveal the first glimmers of a shift in thinking—that she might not have to feel compelled to feel responsible and guilty as an automatic reaction. What might you say to follow-up on this opening?

In this follow-up brief video exchange, the patient again brings the issue of safety into the session. In Part 1, the patient uses a water/shoreline metaphor when she cautiously revealed to the therapist that she feels safe with him—"if I head for the shoals, you will keep me safe."

The current case vignette occurs four months later, when the patient brings in an "awful" dream. Notice that once again, the patient directs us to the themes of safety and vulnerability, self-blame, and dangerous aloneness, only this time the dream symbol of the little boy being at risk is more acutely felt. Now we see that the patient is much more visibly in pain, and we see that she again feels fully responsible, with an urgency to do something.

Please refer to the Routledge website, Video 8.3: Over-idealized Transference, Part 2.

Questions for Discussion

1. The patient says, "The boy was out too far, a wave crashes over him, there was no one to help, and I was all alone." Symbolically, what might the patient be conveying to the therapist?

2. How might we inquire as to whether the patient's more direct and intense emotions emerging through the dream can be applied to the therapy process?

   a. Does the patient feel in over her head?

b. Would you ask about her sense of vulnerability?

3. When the patient reverts to painful self-blame, the therapist asks if there was a lifeguard. Explain how this question might help to counteract the patient's self-blame?

4. Notice that the therapist then asks how old the patient was in the dream. This question was intended to validate her internal struggle and to not leave her to deal with the conflict alone. What do you make of the patient's immediate moment of avoidance and withdrawal?

5. The therapist is directing her back to not pressuring herself, reflecting that this was too much responsibility to take on, as she was a young person herself. What do you make of the patient's moment of defensiveness and withdrawal?

6. After the patient reports that she wants to move away from the topic because she is visibly upset, the therapist asks if it feels safe talking about this in here. (His comment is a delicate inquiry into the issue of safety, a form of palpating the transference.) Notice that the patient deflects the therapist's question. At this juncture, do you think that the therapist is making a helpful intervention or not so helpful?

   a. Explain why it might be a good example of therapeutic tracking, probing into the relationship between responsibility and safety?

   b. Explain why the patient's reaction may be an indication of the therapist moving too quickly into "forbidden territory" around old loyalty patterns in relation to her father.

> c. How might you intervene differently at this juncture?

The following case vignette illustrates extreme negative transference. This woman has been in treatment for over a year and has had difficulty in many of her relationships, including friendships, her husband, and two former therapists. Here we see the patient's hidden expectations for the therapist "to do some-thing" coming to the surface through the following transferential enactment.

Please refer to the Routledge website, Video 8.4: Negative Transference.

Questions for Discussion

1. What are your reactions to the therapist's initial statements in response to the patient's frustration?

   a. When he reflects back to her the question, "It seems like I'm not listening?"

   b. The tone of the therapist's voice, his body language, and his general state of calm?

2. The patient essentially is saying that she doesn't think he's listening, he's passively indifferent, and when this happens, she feels invisible. The therapist then invites the patient to look together at what happens for her when he misunderstands her or hurts her and wonders what might be getting triggered from her past. Explain why this comment escalates the negative transference.

3. The therapist says that he didn't think that he was being defensive, but if she felt that way, he was sorry. She acknowledges that he's not doing this on purpose, but she then brings up the distance again. Question: What might you have said around the theme of distance or disconnection?

4. Instead, the therapist directs her back to her hopelessness, and he invites her back into the present to explain her assumptions that he's "like the rest of them." He then makes reference to her statement that therapy with anyone is a dead-end street, and again directs her back to her own feelings. She then says, "Aren't you supposed to know what to do with me in these situations?" Again, the therapist directs her back to her feelings. Question: What could he have done differently to stay in the present moment with her frustration?

5. Using the Four Quadrant Model:

   a. What is the patient communicating around expectations in Quadrant Three?

   b. How is Quadrant Four being activated around the patient's disappointment?

6. When the therapist asks her to help him understand what he doesn't get, what shift begins to occur in the dynamic?

7. When he asks if this is happening right now, the patient says, "No, not really." This affirmation lets the therapist know that she perhaps feels that he is with her in the present moment and that he is not retaliating in return.

This is a difficult situation for any therapist to find her/himself in. The patient continues to project her own frustration onto the therapist, demanding that he admit that he is capable of making mistakes. She both wants him to be fallible and wants him to know what to do, to read her mind even when she doesn't actively express frustration. This episode was triggered by her disappointment and discouragement that the therapist didn't pick up on her frustration with their relationship, a comment she had made in passing two sessions ago.

We would agree that the therapist indeed should have initiated inquiry about her frustration, even if it meant interrupting her from "going on and on about her sister's flirting." This case example illustrates why tracking transferential statements and, when possible, palpating comments that convey disappointment in the relational alliance are very important. If the therapist had done so, possibly the patient's intense reaction would not have erupted as it did in this video.

In any case, the eruption of Quadrant Four retaliation and accusations around the therapist's competence does require a steadiness on the therapist's part. The patient's greatest fear is that the therapist will retaliate in return, and the distance between them would increase even further. This fear/assumption on the patient's part is what was at least partially prevented in this session. Although difficult, and less than optimal in the tracking, the steady non-defensiveness of the therapist allowed for a shift to occur in the relationship as well as the patient's internal state. This is also how the eruption of Quadrant Four negative transference can be viewed as a potential sign that the authentic self can begin to emerge if formerly taboo expressions can be uttered without damaging effects to the overall relationship.

In this next video, we see an example of the patient at an ending point in therapy. We see the patient able to reflect upon her evolving relationship with the therapist, shifting from over-idealization (old hopes and dreams around rescue) to shifting into feeling a more equal partner in the therapy relationship. This is an example of how Quadrant Three resolves itself.

However, this is not a linear process. While the patient can acknowledge her growth and appreciate a more equalized relationship, she also immediately brings up sadness and grief over her old longings (for rescue) never being actualized. Yet being able to feel these longings much more fully, the patient is now able to see beyond her restrictive idealizations and progressively own her emerging health. The reasons why she needed to create her idealizations at a painful time of her life come into much clearer focus, including the role they played in helping her to survive. Notice the number and nature of the questions that the therapist uses in this case vignette to help identify entrenched loyalty standards in Quadrant Three.

Please refer to the Routledge website, Video 8.5: The Role of Transference in Relationship Consolidation.

Questions for Discussion

1. *As a way of validating the relational and systemic gains the patient has made from her pre-existing idealizations, the therapist acknowledges the distance she has come in differentiating between her self-confirming health and her self-denying loyalty systems. It is at this time that the therapist asks to hear more about the sadness she has mentioned. Why does the therapist mark sadness at this time?*

2. *Bringing up sadness allows the patient to talk more directly about her old hopes and dreams. Validating her old hopes, the therapist then points out how having the courage to own her deep sadness has allowed her the many changes she has made, like a switch being flipped inside. How would you explain the power that this validation of her longings had in connection to the patient's growth?*

3. *The patient is then able to shift to feeling her disappointments with her father. This leads to a flash of memory—she asks something of her father, he says no, saying he was doing this for the good of her family. She feels guilty and puts him on a pedestal. Here the therapist senses feelings of shame hiding behind the patient's attempts to put her father on a pedestal. He validates her grave disappointment by saying it wasn't a two-way street, thus addressing her still-unacknowledged feelings of shame.*

    a. *Discuss how the comment around unfairness leads to the redefining of loyalty standards?*

    b. *We assume the patient's hidden shame would be around having needs of her own. Can hidden shame be alleviated without mentioning the word?*

4. *The therapist connects the patient's previous loyalty to her father with avoiding her feelings of disappointment and avoiding her anger at him. He then contextualizes this to the present moment by validating her growing feelings of equality in the treatment situation. Explain how allowing for the experience of negative feeling states contributes to the emergence of the real self.*

SUMMARY OF TRANSFERENCE

When transference can be seen as a fluctuating enactment, the moment-to-moment tracking in any session becomes far more productive. The more process-oriented the treatment, the easier it becomes to "see" fluctuating enactments in the transference. Among other components, the consciousness of patients is tied to mood, stress, and to both a relational and intrapsychic context. What was non-conscious a moment ago may become conscious now, and as we have noted, the situation can reverse itself. Note also that the distance between past and present is markedly reduced in this process. Put differently, the phenomenological present encompasses the past in the inter-systemic present.

We see positive and negative transference developing throughout treatment. Within such tracking, we see that positive and negative can reverse themselves at any time in either direction. As a result we can also confirm for ourselves that positive and negative transferences are two sides of the same coin. What was once hopeful through idealized expectations can quickly flip to a negative transferential reaction when disappointment shatters hope for rescue or acknowledgment. Neither positive transference nor negative transference can be adequately understood if they are looked at independently of each other. Dissociated elements of negative appear in the positive, and dissociated elements of the positive appear in the negative. Each is subjectively alive, but their "disconnected connection" only yields to resolution through the treatment process itself.

We have stressed that working with transference places us at the cutting edge of emergence. For example, properly understood and properly handled, negative transference is a dynamic force for personality integration. By palpating negative transferential communication as it emerges, we prevent more extreme responses from threatening the alliance. An unfolding authenticity supersedes the compulsive need to care for others, or to override others, or avoid others.

The rewards of working with transferential feelings are enormous. As the therapeutic encounter goes deeper, it allows for greater honesty and authentic expression. In particular, hidden and often paralyzing shame is faced, processed, and integrated, such that the dismantling of non-conscious organizing schemas becomes possible.

We have also stressed that transference operationalizes the Four Quadrant Model such that all four quadrants can be activated at any given moment, or they may be activated simultaneously. As an enactment creates its vibrations across the entire process grid, the therapeutic task becomes one of monitoring, understanding, and ultimately engaging these vibrations. For example, patients with difficulties asserting themselves will often form a painful pattern of loyally waiting for the therapist to provide a magical cure. Of course *all* the quadrants are engaged, but the dynamics of loyal waiting are most visible in Quadrant Three, with increasing reverberations in all the other quadrants as disappointment mounts.

The therapeutic task of working with transference is greatly aided by our capacity to maintain a holding environment that sustains our therapeutic alliance. A holding environment in turn depends on understanding the timing of when and how to comment on the patient's defensive structure. In this regard, optimal use of language, especially in finding entry points, can invite curiosity and can also *forecast* a theme or issue before it fully emerges into consciousness. Language can be used to *slow down* an overly rapid dialogue to invite deeper inquiry and a deeper confidence in being held safely.

SELF-REFLECTION QUESTIONS FOR OVERALL REVIEW: TRANSFERENCE AND THE THERAPEUTIC HOLDING ENVIRONMENT

As a conclusion to our chapter on transference, we leave you with several generic questions on the topic. Each question is meant to generate thought and discussion around the challenges of this topic.

Questions: Understanding Transference as a Dimension of the Therapeutic Holding Environment

1. Are supportive comments always holding? If not, when are they not?

---

2. What is the difference between therapeutic holding and positive transference?

3. How does one determine when it would be too soon to make a verbal observation or reflection?

4. How is therapeutic holding related to phenomenological tracking in the present moment?

5. When is silence helpful, and when can it create a rupture of attunement?

6. How might loyal waiting interfere with internalizing the promising aspects of the holding environment created by the therapist?

7. How does a history of violations of trust confound the clinical issue of loyal waiting?

Questions: Using Transference in the Service of Integration

1. What burdens do positive and negative transference place on the therapist?

2. How is listening for what's not being said a safeguard against the eruption of full-blown negative transference or premature termination of therapy?

3. *Discuss why negative transference is not a sign of failed treatment. In other words, how is the emergence of negative transference a critical part of therapy?*

4. *Discuss how positive and negative transference can be palpated by using the Four Quadrant Model.*

9

Consolidation of Gains
Resilience Rediscovered

The intersubjective field of the analysis, made possible by the emotional availability of both analyst and patient, becomes a developmental second chance for the patient.
—Orange, Atwood, and Stolorow (1997, p. 8)

Unless the therapist is willing to bring her authentic self into the room, the patient may end up analyzed—but never found.
—Stark (1999, p. xxii.)

[Real Self] engenders the spontaneity of feelings, whether these be joy, yearning, love, anger, fear, despair. It also is the source of spontaneous interests and energies—it is the part of ourselves that wants to expand and grow and to fulfill itself—this indicates that our real self, when strong and active, enables us to make decisions and assume responsibility for them. It therefore leads to genuine integration and a sound sense of wholeness, oneness. Not merely are body and mind, deed and thought or feeling, consonant and harmonious, but they function without serious inner conflict.
—Horney (1950, p. 157)

Karen Horney's succinct description of the real self describes an integrated personality, one that is able to feel the full spectrum of emotions, a self that is spontaneous, responsible, and without serious inner conflict. The relational position and availability of the therapist, as Orange, Atwood, Stolorow, and Stark point out, is an integral component in the mix of what makes for a successful psychotherapy.

For the patient, the measure of a successful therapy involves the capacity to function without serious inner conflict. This is what we all hope to achieve with patients at the end of a successful therapy. Although we typically associate the processes of integration and consolidation with the ending phase of treatment, "micro-consolidations" or glimmers of the authentic self occur throughout the therapeutic journey.

Emergent aspects of the real self are often difficult to spot in the early phases of treatment. The difficulty in recognizing and consolidating initial gains is due in part to the fact that they are often "swallowed-up" or undone by reflexive attempts to preserve the old homeostatic balance of the character solution. We are reminded that this is the "habituated nature" of character organization, that is, a child's early adaptive attempts to achieve self-regulation and a sense of self-worth.

As we have stated throughout this text, the dismantling of compulsively driven character solutions is not a linear process. For every forward movement, an unconscious recoil effect is likely to follow, until gradually changes can be metabolized into the core of the authentic self. Learned characterological solutions fight therapeutic gains as if they were "a threat to their existence." This is because each characterological solution is *itself* a tightly woven systemic whole, "comfortable" because of its familiarity and rescue potential, even if unwanted or painful.

However, remaining in the present allows us to see how the past and present are intertwined. And we can only consolidate a gain in the present moment through tracking the dynamic process. This is how the real self gradually emerges over time. The tracking process clearly involves a complicated tug of war between health and non-health. Any gain around self-emergence is bound to create a backlash as dissociative mechanisms seek to revert to the old homeostatic balance.

THE THERAPEUTIC CHANGE PROCESS

We have all experienced therapeutic gains, in ourselves and in our patients. Whether small or large, they strike a different inner feeling and sense of ourselves. And once we have internalized even a bit of these gains, we cannot be talked out of them. As has been said, only partly in jest, the only thing that cannot be analyzed in our patients is their health!

In this text, we have made a clear distinction between health and non-health, not only in theory, but also in the moment-to-moment phenomenological tracking of each dynamic in real time. By tracking health and non-health simultaneously, we enhance our listening capacities to see, hear, feel, and sense the tender tendrils of the authentic self as it faces internal conflict. It is through this process that patients progressively gain strength in uncovering their inherent resilience.

Tracking this non-linear change process requires the development of a "listening ear" on the part of the therapist—a type of listening that is able to catch burgeoning signs of growth. When the therapist is able to catch the micro-emergence of the real self as it unfolds in the present moment, then these emergent signs of heath are able to be reflected back to the patient.

Once the therapist recognizes the pull between health and stasis, the nuances of the internal war being waged, the therapist can strive to protect glimmers of change or progress by mirroring them back to the patient, thus reinforcing and solidifying the "realness" of what just occurred dynamically. This mirroring allows the therapist to highlight the patient's inherent constructive forces that have been "dormant," lying in wait for the proper moment to emerge.

Just as gains are ongoing in treatment, the consolidation of gains is occurring the moment a patient arrives in our office. Treatment gains and consolidation of them are therefore part of a larger system very much alive in the therapeutic process. This emergence occurs because of the relational safety created throughout the treatment. Thus, seizing upon the opportunity to comment upon and support gains, even if seemingly small, marks a relational and dynamic change. An "important other" is there to celebrate accomplishments in an emerging real self, thus uncovering the resilient core that has been waiting for recognition, validation, and acceptance.

CONSOLIDATION OF GAINS: EXAMPLES THROUGHOUT TREATMENT

The first case is an example of early signs of the real self breaking through. Notice how each glimmer of emergence is quickly followed by statements from the patient where she cancels out or diminishes herself, reasserting the old standards around performance and perfectibility. However, the therapist continues to support and encourage tentative signs of growth. This illustrates how the therapist's mirroring of emerging signs of health can continue to be internalized, both interpersonally and intrapsychically.

Please refer to the Routledge website, Video 9.1: Early Consolidation of Gains.

Questions for Discussion

1. *At the beginning of this vignette, the patient is able to articulate her growing awareness of the parts of her husband that he kept hidden from her. When the therapist asks how the patient is feeling about these insights, she says, "I feel like a stupid jerk." How would you explain what occurred in that moment?*

2. *What does the therapist do to help the patient modify her harshness and steer her back to connections that the patient made, reinforcing how important they were?*

   a. *In terms of fairness to herself versus to her husband?*

---

b. In terms of beating herself up for not seeing something earlier?

3. *The patient's fear of offending others is then juxtaposed against the patient's opportunity to speak the truth. This is a central conflict that is beginning to surface in the treatment. Track what the therapist tries to do to help integrate this split throughout the remainder of this vignette.*

4. *There is a shift that occurs where the patient is able to describe her sense of self, articulating that she feels like a "jellyfish" or fears "becoming unglued" if she offends others and they abandon her. However, the patient is also able to articulate the parts of her that are solid. Discuss how this shifting back and forth between feeling like a jellyfish and feeling like a good person is a sign of growing self-acknowledgment.*

5. *What are your thoughts about the therapist volunteering what she sees as the patient's core strengths?*

6. *When the therapist invites the patient to say more about her core strengths, notice the backlash that occurs when the patient identifies her empathy toward others and chastises herself for not doing something to help. What other statements could you have made to the patient at this time?*

7. *The therapist identifies the need to "do something" as emanating from the patient's childhood and placing a pretty big weight on her shoulders. Identify what the patient does in response.*

Analysis and Commentary

Often patients with perfectionistic expectations stemming from childhood rely on adult support that was inconsistent or unreliable. In treatment, they tend to chastise themselves following a breakthrough of authentic insight. It is as if saying, "Why wasn't I able to see this from the beginning?" Feelings of self-hate and recrimination will threaten to undo earlier gains in treatment. However, this video exchange is an example of how the therapist's steady encouragement supports emerging health and resilience within the dialogue, allowing consolidation of gains to take place.

In this second case vignette, the patient is talking with his therapist about coming out to his parents. In prior sessions, the patient presented with acute feelings of shame when he was struggling with finding the courage to admit to his therapist that he was gay. After working on the transferential fears, the patient was now ready to face his parents directly. Notice the extremes in language the patient uses when he anticipates what the experience will be like. The therapist helps track by engaging in a *rehearsal* of imagining what he might say in an effort to help calm fears of losing his family.

Please refer to the Routledge website, Video 9.2: Emerging Authenticity.

Questions for Discussion

1. How would you work with the patient's extremes in language at the beginning of the vignette?

2. Point out ways in which the therapist used entry point tracking to help the patient articulate more of who he is.

3. The therapist identifies the pressure that the patient puts on himself to "say it just right." How might you explore that pressure in greater detail?

4. The therapist then reflects the "double bind" within which the patient is caught—his fear of losing his family and the fear of not being able to

> show the world who he really is. How might you explore similar dilemmas with your own patients around feeling double bound?
>
> 5. The therapist directs the patient back to how he felt in the session when he "rehearsed" coming out. The patient said he felt relief, and the therapist mirrored that back to him. However, she reminded him that there are no guarantees that this would go that well with his parents. Why is it important to articulate "no guarantees" in situations such as these?
>
> 6. Notice that the therapist helped the patient think of other supports to rely on if his family rejects his news. How does that help consolidate gains around personal growth and authenticity?

This next vignette is a continuation of the case history of sexual abuse that was presented in Chapter 7. Notice the progress around the consolidation regarding levels of integrating the reality of what happened to him in childhood. It is not uncommon for individuals to experience levels of integration followed by the readjustment and integration of expanding organizing schemas with regard to self and other. Often after seeing one phase of consolidation, the therapeutic process will be followed by a period of *respite* that allows for further integration to occur. This session takes place approximately eight months after the earlier three-part session segment.

Please refer to the Routledge website, Video 9.3: Continuing Integration around the Reality of Abuse.

Patient: I keep going back to a phrase you said to me last week. You know, when something hits you in a really deep place? That phrase was like a bell tone that kept running through my head. I couldn't stop hearing your words. When you said, "These things happened to you." It was so simple, but it really penetrated.

Therapist: Why do you think these words impacted you so?

Patient: It's like holding a thread. We've spent so much time focusing on my abuse, and I've worked a lot of it through. But, there's first order abuse, and there's second order of abuse as well.

Therapist: Second order abuse?

Patient: You know, all of what happened to me. There's the abuse, but then there are the messages that I internalized. They said, "We're going to kill you if you don't keep quiet." "We can take you whenever we want." And I think that I started to believe that I mean nothing; I'm not worth much, a thing to be used.

Therapist: And then you learned to overcompensate to try to prove them wrong.

Patient: Yeah, I became a fighter and a doer, but I don't want to fight anymore. I don't want to try so hard anymore

Therapist: I'm thinking back to our last session and what it was that made me say that phrase last week. You came in, and you told me that you had become aware of "a part of yourself" that still didn't believe that these things really happened to you. I'm wondering if my phrase spoke to that part . . . spoke to that part that still held the hidden belief that you weren't worth very much, and the only way you could protect yourself from that belief was to not completely take in that the abuse really happened.

Patient: Yes, the shame and feeling worthless was the part of the experience that went underground. It was the part without language, or unconscious, that happened as a result of what they did to me. When you acknowledged that this really happened, it let me have an experience of a real human being, right here in the present moment, you heard me, almost like a witness.

Therapist: Almost like we brought the full experience, past and present, into the room in the present moment?

Patient: Yes, yes. That's exactly it. The more the past reality is acknowledged, the easier it is to enter the present moment. (Long pause) That feels like consolidation . . . a bit like holding both ends of something at the same time. (Pause) I'm glad I said that because they're all part of me. I just can't throw out the past.

Therapist: No, you can't. But in talking about it, the past changes a bit, or the impact of the past changes.

Patient: Yeah, I'm aware that when something triggers me, I'm less inclined to fight back, to get even. By implication, I guess that makes me less reactive. (Pause, and a smile) I'm feeling pretty good right now. I see how a lot of the pieces past and present fit together.

Therapist: I think you said it beautifully earlier. Things are consolidating.

Patient: Right. I'm still in the process, but I don't need to fix it. I just need to live it.

Analysis

When the therapist asks for clarification of "second order abuse," the patient is able to articulate that "I mean nothing; I'm not worth much, a thing to be used." The therapist then connects this to her patient's strategy of learning to overcompensate in an effort not to feel that worthless. The patient agrees, saying he learned to be a fighter and a doer. He adds that he no longer wishes to expend that amount of effort in "proving himself" to the world. Here we see how the patient is able to connect his conscious awareness of feelings of worthlessness with his strategy of overcompensation. It is only when he is able to make this connection consciously that he is able to relinquish the reflexive, protective strategy.

Notice that the therapist then reflects on what made her reinforce the phrase, "These things happened to you." She is able to remember that the patient said that a part of himself still didn't believe these things happened to him. By remembering this sequence himself, the patient is then able to access hidden feelings of shame more directly. Here, the therapist illustrates how the past and the present come into the room simultaneously as the integration process further consolidates.

In this next case vignette, the patient had been working with her therapist for several years. She has made steady gains around affect-regulation in her communication exchanges with her self-absorbed partner. Here she gives voice to the consolidation of gains made in treatment as she describes with clarity her partner's character.

Please refer to the Routledge website, Video 9.4: Ending a Relationship.

Patient:	I've been noticing that I'm just not worked up anymore about my relationship with Alan. Nothing he does or doesn't do in his own therapy matters to me . . . because he's not changing, or I should say he's not changing significantly enough. (Pause) I don't know if he can. You know, I was telling my friend that Alan is like a hollow Easter Bunny. He's empty in the middle. There's no solid core.
Therapist:	Empty in the middle. (Smiles) What a great analogy.
Patient:	I don't know if that's fair, but I think it's true. You know, just like those hollow Easter Bunnies, all shiny gold foil on the outside, that's the image he presents to the world. And that's what everyone sees, which is why he's able to charm people. But, if you give him a strong poke, your finger goes right through. And it doesn't take much. (Pause) I think I'm different. I have a core. It may have been a damaged core, but it's solid.
Therapist:	And we've done a lot of work on repairing and healing that core.
Patient:	There's too much of a gap between us. His childhood was so damaging. Even if that hollowness is filling in slowly, I think we have

too much baggage. I don't hate him. I've given all that up; I've let that go with the help that you've given me in here. Now I find that being angry with him, even hoping that he will change, takes too much energy. I guess that why I can forgive him.

Therapist: So you feel that you have forgiven him at this point?

Patient: Yes. But, I don't trust him. I don't even like him anymore. I certainly don't respect him, but I can forgive him because I understand how fragile he really is.

Therapist: You're able to connect his distancing behavior and his affair with his fragility.

Patient: Yes, and that's why he can't get me worked up anymore.

Therapist: And it sounds like you are able to understand the reality of how long it might take before he will be able to make changes that are significant enough that they would impact your level of intimacy.

Patient: Yes, yes. And I see more clearly how we're not even on the same page in terms of our values, what's important to each of us. You have to have some shared value system if there's going to be any real connection on a day-to-day basis. (Pause) If I were really honest with myself, I don't think Alan has the ability to be a couple. (Pause) I think the point is that I'm not holding onto any hope anymore. Initially, I agreed to do couples' counseling because I wanted to believe there was hope. But he's not ready to be a couple; he's barely a self.

Therapist: Essentially, that insight is what you gained by doing the couples' therapy, even though I know it was terribly frustrating and disappointing to you.

Patient: Yes, clarity through another disappointment. You know, I sometimes look back over all the time I spent in this marriage. And I get upset with myself, upset about making some of the decisions I did—to stay, to give him another chance. But I'm not kicking myself for that anymore because going through this with you in therapy allowed me to have so much more understanding about myself. I'm actually grateful in a funny kind of way.

Therapist: Yes?

Patient: The journey would have turned out so differently. If I had ended the relationship years ago, I would have short-changed myself. This process helped me grow into the person I am now. I never realized that when I started.

Analysis

This is a case example near the end of a treatment process. The patient is able to clearly differentiate what it feels like to have a solid core and how she is now better able to assess whether others possess a hollow core or a solid one. Notice that she has let go of her former wish (contained in Quadrant Three), where she loyally waited for her partner to change. She reflects upon the hope that somehow her own diligent efforts might have been able to change him. The patient reveals that these unrealistic wishes and longings are no longer a part of who she is.

Having let go of over-idealized wishes and longings, she is also able to reflect upon her ability to let go of the frustration she felt earlier in the treatment, when Quadrant Four episodes of "lashing out" at him were a frequent manifestation of her disappointment. Now, she is able to see clearly that changing her husband in the marriage is impossible. However, she is also able to forgive him because she is aware of his limitations and brokenness.

Finally, rather than being derailed by regret for having "wasted" so much time in the marriage waiting for him to change, she is able to reflect that her own therapy process allowed her to grow into the person she is today. Here, the patient exhibits healthy signs of authentic self-worth and sense of accomplishment.

The fifth vignette captures a therapeutic exchange later in the treatment process. This patient had struggled for years with issues around self-esteem and self-differentiation. The daughter of a distant father and narcissistically cold and critical mother, this patient repeatedly put others' needs ahead of her own. In addition, she presented with a style of self-effacement and humor as a way of hiding her feelings of both anger and disappointment in others.

This dialogue between the patient and therapist illustrates the back-and-forth struggle the patient experiences between expressing her anger and doubting her right to do so. What we see in this session is an example of how "permission-giving" and *slowing the process down* at a point of potential consolidation help the patient get in touch with deeply buried feelings of sadness. She clearly feels compassion for the little girl who worked so hard to please others all of her life. This connection to sadness and self-compassion is part of how the loyalty bind begins to shift for this patient.

Please refer to the Routledge website, Video 9.5: Later Consolidation of Gains.

Questions for Discussion

1. *The patient begins the session by reporting on how she was able to express anger and let people know how she was feeling. However, she wonders whether she handled it correctly. The therapist reflects that the patient is critiquing herself harshly if she thinks she is not doing things perfectly. How does this help curtail the backlash of over-determined efforts?*

2. *What do you make of the therapist's comment of saying that the patient has "every right" to create distance?*

3. *How does the therapist demonstrate moment-to-moment tracking of the patient's feelings around distancing and fears around creating too much distance?*

4. *When the patient begins to cry as she experiences the pain of the little girl, the therapist supports the compassion that is developing for that little girl as well. How does this help challenge the perfectionistic standards?*

5. *How does the therapist challenge the patient's "self-analysis" when the patient dismisses her anger at Helen as a projection of feelings toward her mother?*

6. *How does the patient then demonstrate a growing sense of self-confidence?*

7. *Describe what the friend, Helen, was trying to do at the end of their conversation? What does this say about individuation and merger?*

8. *How does the therapist work with the "confusion" around merger and sameness?*

9. *How do you assess the moments when the patient says, "Wait a minute, let me tell you about this first."*

a. Does it break the momentum from deeper exploration?

b. Does the break help the patient with regulating the pace of her integration?

10. Discuss the symbolic importance of the white board in the dream in terms of helping the consolidation process.

Analysis and Commentary

This case vignette was selected to help illustrate the back-and-forth process that occurs between expressions of self-assertion and doubts about how to hold onto less familiar, though stronger, expressions of the self. Notice how the patient expresses uncertainty after every assertion, often remarking that "none of this makes sense" or "I'm not being very clear." One of the ways that the therapist gently holds and tracks the unfolding process is by reflecting that what the patient is saying is clear, that it does make sense, and that she has a right to have strong feelings in the present moment without them being diminished as projections or reenactments of the past. In later phases of treatment, this reassurance through active mirroring of the patient's emerging self is at the core of consolidating further gains.

As an ending to this chapter, we are reintroducing a video that summarizes the entire learning points of the Workbook. You have seen clips or segments of this throughout the various chapters.

This 30-minute video is a consultation summary of one therapist's consolidation of her own gains around understanding how to apply the Four Quadrant Model to her work. We hope that it serves as a consolidation for your own gains as well.

Please refer to the Routledge website, Video 9.6: Summary of Learning Points.

SUMMARY

Consolidation of gains is an ongoing process in therapy. This is because change itself is ongoing. Change is neither sequential nor linear, nor is it episodic. Rather, it is an evolving dynamic that can be tracked moment-to-moment and experienced as it unfolds.

In the early stages of treatment, it is the therapist who is more likely to be the one able to register and track mini-gains and micro-movements toward health. As treatment progresses, the patient also becomes gradually more able to stay with emerging health. We might say that the patient is moving from crutches to a cane!

What "listening energy" is required to be able to identify and support constructive signs in the space between patient and therapist, a space that is often now called the "intersubjective" space? This intersubjective space allows deeper levels of attunement with the patient as well as a deeper process on the part of the therapist to consciously monitor personal emotional triggers. Therefore, the "listening energy" that we speak of involves the following:

- The capacity and freedom to immerse oneself in the patient's struggles, conflicts, longings, and relationally and psychically based organizing schemas.
- Once familiar with these patterns, the therapist is better equipped to "listen for" emerging signs of change, even if those shifts are momentary and thereafter easily undone.
- When these momentary shifts toward authenticity begin to emerge, it is the therapist's task to make note of the shift, highlighting the significance of even small steps toward growth.

We have found that one of the reasons this form of "listening energy" is difficult to master is that many therapists fear they will become absorbed in the patient's struggles and be unable to extricate themselves, once they are more fully involved. Therapists also fear that "recoil effects" following healthier steps forward may be a bad omen. However, once we are able to resonate with our own fears, the process becomes less fraught. Therapeutic confidence builds as the therapist begins to see how the process creates a stronger therapeutic alliance with the patient. As patient trust (and therapist trust!) deepens, engagement and greater degrees of change become possible.

But what if we cannot extricate ourselves from compelling struggles and patient conflicts? Issues of class, gender, and race can complicate our understanding of the "space" between us. But even without such demographic factors, the therapeutic process can hardly itself proceed without at some point the patient "transferring" feelings, thoughts, or motives to the therapist.

Transference becomes utterly common as does counter-transference. But this is only technical language for what happens over a period of time in *every* intimate relationship. It becomes important to recognize that nothing is "bad" in psychotherapy, neither transference nor counter-transference. In a sense, witnessing the emergence of transferential feelings is a doorway through which we can begin to reform and repair relational misattunements or develop more secure relational attachments in the present moment through the therapeutic relationship. The classic example of this is the emergence of "negative transference."

Negative transference is frequently a breakthrough and indicates the patient trusts us enough to have the courage to complain. This is worth contemplating. Once we are able to see negative transference as a "gain" in terms of trust and safety to express once forbidden thoughts or feelings, a negative transference loses much of its dread. Instead, it can positively energize us in further meaningful engagement. Even with substantially idealized solutions or hidden wishes for retaliation, we bear in mind that the entire construction is the patient's attempt to find a voice, to express needs, to find safety and consistency, and to communicate what hurts in order that feelings of aloneness and isolation can be penetrated and repaired.

Much of what is known as the dynamics of the present (or the dynamics of the here-and-now) is a therapeutic reminder that every moment in treatment has the potential for goodness and truth. And it is the development of our listening energy that allows us to identify and access both visible and hidden constructive forces as these forces emerge in our work. This is at the heart of the theoretical underpinnings of consolidation of gains. Therefore, consolidation of gains may be viewed as a whole series of repeated acts of relational micro-attunement each step along the therapeutic journey. Our bearing witness to these small steps eventually creates major points of integration and further emergence of the resilience of the authentic self.

Epilogue

A ROCK

By Pamela Wallace

My daughter called me her rock the other day, but really, I am only a rock because she is a river.

All those little eddies and undercurrents and flippity floppity fish tails. That churning water, the breathless rapids, the unexpected falling, the jolts, the rolling and clamor of pebble upon pebble, the constant swish, and all the days we spent moving through and across and with the earth together—this is what has taught me strength; this is what has shaped me.

It is neither the rock nor the river that's made me strong, but the relationship between the two.

The kind of strength a rock has is admirable, of course. It is immoveable and always and constant, changing only the way it looks—painted in old age by golden moss, or feathered briefly by a landed bird. And yes, it can be reshaped, but only after generations. It can be moved, but only by external force. What defines the fieldstone is that it remains. You can count on it. It lives always on one side of the fence or the other; it often is the fence, the wall, the thing we stand behind or hunker down with or have to climb over to get beyond. Standing in this particular field, staring at this particular rock, strength looks like something solid and steadfast—a state that is constant and true.

But I'm pretty sure whatever strength I have has come not from constancy, but by constant change. It's not by overcoming and getting past the thing— but by living with the thing. It's living with the thing that over time brings us somewhere new, and makes us stronger. I suspect that resilience is kinder to our souls than steadfastness, and closer to a living love. Because resilience is always relational—it adapts and takes in new information and keeps looking closely—and through that relationship, it becomes stronger. The rock just sits there waiting for something to happen. For you to return. It's kind of a one-way street, kind of a monologue—an impermeable, isolated hunk committed to only one thing—staying put.

Resilience breathes and opens and receives. It takes in; it feels. It's not a you-can-do-this resistance challenge that braces itself for the next onslaught with straightened shoulders and clenching fists. Nor does it hoist itself across great distances to come out "better" on the other side. It's a continual, ongoing, ever-moving current of togetherness; of the thing in the world that bends us, and our own gradual understanding that we haven't been broken at all.

That's the beautiful thing about resilience; as we get better at it, we are actually creating new pathways in our brains. We start to understand that what used to be doesn't always have to be. This seems a more valuable framing than viewing strength as a hard-won truth—as a static, heroic, immoveable, if steadfast, state. Who in the world can maintain THAT high bar? The truth is we will be bent, by grief or loss or trauma—so low we almost break. But we'll never know how much we can withstand until the wind brings us to our knees. And after many, many storms, once we finally realize we're still standing, a new way of being can now enter our consciousness.

It's in relationship where we become strong and where resilience grows. What strengthens us is our capacity to spring back from great disappointment or from crushing loss so that someday we can flow around obstacles, or allow the obstacles to flow around us. I know that after many years, I'm a better mom than I was when I began. At one point I may have wanted my daughter to see me as a rock, but now she knows the truth of it—that I bend, but don't break. And she is better for that knowledge.

So I may be your rock, Olivia, but together, we've become stronger than that. We've become resilient. We are river and rock and an unexpected free fall—and the glittering, deepening stillness of love.

References

Atwood, G. E., & Stolorow, R. D. (2014). *Structures of Subjectivity: Explorations in Psychoanalytic Phenomenology and Contextualism*. New York: Routledge.

Bateman, A., & Fonagy, P. (2008). 8-Year Follow-up of Patients Treated for Borderline Personality Disorder: Mentalization-Based Treatment versus Treatment as Usual. *American Journal of Psychiatry*, *165*, 631–638.

Beck, A. T. (1975). *Cognitive Therapy and the Emotional Disorders*. Madison, CT: International Universities Press.

Bernstein, E. M., & Putnam, F. W. (1986). Development, Reliability, and Validity of a Dissociation Scale. *Journal of Nervous and Mental Disease*, *174*, 727–724.

Cooper, A. M. (1987). Changes in Psychoanalytic Ideas: Transference Interpretation. *Journal of the American Psychoanalytic Association*, *35*, 77–98.

Cozolino, L. (2012). *The Neuroscience of Psychotherapy: Healing the Social Brain* (2nd ed.). New York: Norton.

Courtois, C. A., & Ford, J. D. eds. (2009). *Treating Complex Traumatic Stress Disorders: An Evidence-Based Guide*. New York: Guilford Press.

Crastnopol, M. (2015). *Micro-Trauma: A Psychoanalytic Understanding of Cumulative Psychic Injury*. New York: Routledge.

Curtis, R. C. (2014). Systematic Research Supporting Psychoanalytic and Psychodynamic *Treatments. Contemporary Psychoanalysis*, *50*(1–2), 34–42.

Danielian, J., & Gianotti, P. (2012). *Listening with Purpose: Entry Points into Shame and Narcissistic Vulnerability*. Lanham, MD: Jason Aronson.

Dearing, R. L., & Tangney, J. P. eds. (2011). *Shame in the Therapy Hour*. Washington, DC: American Psychological Association.

DeRosis, L. (1974). The Invented Self: Karen Horney's Theory Applied to Psychoanalysis in Groups. *The American Journal of Psychoanalysis*, *34*, 109–121.

DeYoung, P. A. (2015). *Understanding and Treating Shame: A Relational/Neurobiological Approach*. New York: Routledge.

Ferenczi, S. (1926, 1994). *Further Contributions to the Theory and Technique of Psychoanalysis*, ed. J. Rickman (orig. publ. Hogarth, 1926). London: Karnac.

Fonagy, P. (2015). The Effectiveness of Psychodynamic Psychotherapies: An Update. *World Psychiatry, 14*(2), 137–150.

Fonagy, P., Rost, F., Carlyle, J., McPherson, S., Thomas, R., Pasco Fearon, R. M., Goldberg, D., & Taylor, D. (2015). Pragmatic Randomized Controlled Trial of Long-Term Psychoanalytic Psychotherapy for Treatment-Resistant Depression: The Tavistock Adult Depression Study. *World Psychiatry*, *14*(3), 312–321.

Fosha, D. (2000). *The Transformative Power of Affect: A Model of Accelerated Change*. New York: Basic Books.

Fosha, D. (2003). Dyadic Regulation and Experiential Work with Emotion and Relatedness in Trauma and Disorganized Attachment. In M. F. Solomon & D. J. Siegel, eds., *Healing Trauma: Attachment, Mind, Body, and Brain* (Chapter 6, p. 227). New York: Norton.

Geist, R. A. (2008). Connectedness, Permeable Boundaries, and the Development of the Self: Therapeutic Implications. *International Journal of Psychoanalytic Self Psychology, 3*, 129–152.

Ginot, E. (2007). Intersubjectivity and Neuroscience: Understanding Enactments and Their Therapeutic Significance within Emerging Paradigms. *Psychoanalytic Psychology, 24*, 317–332.

Ginot, E. (2009). The Empathic Power of Enactments: The Link between Neuropsychological Processes and an Expanded Definition of Empathy. *Psychoanalytic Psychology, 26*, 290–309.

Heilman, K. M., Nadeau, S. E., & Beversdorf, D. O. (2003). Creative Innovation: Possible Brain Mechanisms. *Neurocase, 9*, 369–379.

Herman, J. (1997). *Trauma and Recovery.* New York: Basic Books.

Horney, K. (1939). *New Ways in Psychoanalysis.* New York: Norton.

Horney, K. (1945). *Our Inner Conflicts: A Constructive Theory of Neurosis.* New York: Norton.

Horney, K. (1950). *Neurosis and Human Growth: The Struggle towards Self-Realization.* New York: Norton.

Horney, K. (1987). *Final Lectures by Karen Horney*, ed. D. H. Ingram. New York: Norton.

Howell, E. F. (2005). *The Dissociative Mind.* New York: Routledge.

Kohut, H. (1966). Forms and Transformations of Narcissism. *Journal of the American Psychoanalytic Association, 14*, 243–272.

Kohut, H. (1977). *The Restoration of the Self.* New York: International Universities Press.

Kohut, H. (1984). *How Does Analysis Cure?* Chicago, IL: University of Chicago Press.

Lazarus, A. A. (1981). *The Practice of Multimodal Therapy.* New York: McGraw-Hill.

Levine, P. A. (2010). *In an Unspoken Voice: How the Body Releases Trauma and Restores Goodness.* Berkeley, CA: North Atlantic Books.

Levine, P. A. (2015). *Trauma and Memory: Brain and Body in a Search for the Living Past: A Practical Guide for Understanding and Working with Traumatic Memory.* Berkeley, CA: North Atlantic Books.

Liotti, G. (1992). Disorganized/Disoriented Attachment in the Etiology of the Dissociative Disorders. *Dissociation, 5*, 196–204.

Liotti, G. (1999). Disorganization of Attachment as a Model for Understanding Dissociative Psychopathology. In J. Solomon & C. George, eds., *Attachment Disorganization* (pp. 291–317). New York: Guilford Press.

Luborsky, L. (1984). *Principles of Psychoanalytic Psychotherapy: A Manual for Supportive-Expressive (SE) Treatment.* New York: Basic Books.

Main, M. (1995). Recent Studies in Attachment: Overview, with Implications for Clinical Work. In S. Goldberg, R. Muir, & J. Kerr, eds., *Attachment Theory: Social, Developmental and Clinical Perspectives* (pp. 407–474). Hillsdale, NJ: Analytic Press.

Neborsky, R. J. (2003). A Clinical Model for the Comprehensive Treatment of Trauma Using an Affect Experiencing-Attachment Theory Approach. In M. F. Solomon & D. J. Siegel, eds., *Healing Trauma: Attachment, Mind, Body, and Brain* (pp. 296–297). New York: Norton.

Orange, D. M., Atwood, G. E., & Stolorow, R. D. (1997). *Working Intersubjectively: Contextualism in Psychoanalytic Practice.* Hillsdale, NJ: Analytic Press.

Potter-Effron, R. T. (2011). Therapy with Shame-Prone Alcoholic and Drug-Dependent Clients. In R. L. Dearing & J. P. Tangney, eds., *Shame in the Therapy Hour*. Washington, DC: American Psychological Association.

Putnam, F. W. (1985). Dissociation as a Response to Extreme Trauma. In R. P. Kluft, ed., *The Child Antecedents of Multiple Personality* (pp. 65–97). Washington, DC: American Psychiatric Press.

Rentoul, R. W. (2010). *Ferenczi's Language of Tenderness: Working with Disturbances from the Earliest Years*. Lanham, MD: Jason Aronson.

Russell, E. (2015). *Restoring Resilience: Discovering Your Clients' Capacity for Healing*. New York: Norton.

Scheff, T. J., & Retzinger, S. M. (1991). *Emotions and Violence: Shame and Rage in Destructive Conflicts*. Lincoln, NE: iUniverse, Inc.

Schore, A. N. (1996). Effects of a Secure Attachment Relationship on Right Brain *Development*, Affect Regulation and Infant Mental Health. *Infant Mental Health Journal*, *22*(1–2), 201–269.

Schore, A. N. (2011). The Right Brain Implicit Self lies at the Core of Psychoanalysis. *Psychoanalytic Dialogues: The International Journal of Relational Perspectives*, *21*, 75–100.

Schore, A. N., & Schore, J. (2012). Modern Attachment Theory: The Central Role of Affect Regulation in Development and Treatment. In A. Schore, ed., *The Science of the Art of Psychotherapy* (pp. 27–33). New York: Norton.

Sheldon, J. (2010). The Efficiency of Psychodynamic Psychotherapy. *American Psychologist*, *65*(2), 98–109.

Siegel, D. J. (2003). An Interpersonal Neurobiology of Psychotherapy: The Developing Mind and the Resolution of Trauma. In M. F. Solomon & D. J. Siegel, eds., *Healing Trauma: Attachment, Mind, Body, and Brain* (pp. 3–16). New York: Norton.

Spiegel, D. (1990). Hypnosis, Dissociation and Trauma: Hidden and Overt Observers. In J. Singer, ed., *Repression and Dissociation: Implications for Personality Theory, Psychopathology, and Health* (pp. 121–142). Chicago, IL: University of Chicago Press.

Stark, M. (1999). *Modes of Therapeutic Action: Enhancement of Knowledge, Provision of Experience, and Engagement in Relationship*. Lanham, MD: Jason Aronson.

Stern, D. B. (1985). *The Interpersonal World of the Infant*. New York: Basic Books.

Stern, D. B. (1997). *Unformulated Experience: From Dissociation to Imagination in Psychoanalysis*. Hillsdale, NJ: Analytic Press.

Stolorow, R. D. (2013). Intersubjective-Systems Theory: A Phenomenological—Contextualist Psychoanalytic Perspective. *Psychological Dialogues*, *23*(42), 383–389.

Stolorow, R. D., Brandchaft, B., & Atwood, G. E. (1987). *Psychoanalytic Treatment: An Intersubjective Approach*. Hillsdale, NJ: The Analytic Press.

Sullivan, H. S. (1953). *The Interpersonal Theory of Psychiatry*. New York: Norton.

van der Kolk, B. (2014). *The Body Keeps Score: Brain, Mind, and Body in the Healing of Trauma*. New York: Viking.

Wachtel, P. L. (1993). *Therapeutic Communication: Knowing What to Say When*. New York: Guilford Press.

Wachtel, P. L. (2008). *Relational Theory in the Practice of Psychotherapy*. New York: Guilford Press.

REFERENCES

Wachtel, P. L. (2014). *Cyclical Psychodynamics and the Contextual Self*. New York: Routledge.

Whyte, D. (2012). *River Flow: New and Selected Poems*. Excerpt from "The Seven Streams," p. 285. Langley, Washington, DC: Many Rivers Press.

Winnicott, D. W. (1960). Ego Distortion in Terms of True and False Self. In D. W. Winnicott, ed., *The Maturational Processes and the Facilitating Environment (1965)* (pp. 144–146). New York: International Universities Press.

About the Authors

Patricia Gianotti, PsyD, is a licensed psychologist, clinical supervisor, and founding member of Woodland Psychological Services. Dr. Gianotti is a seasoned lecturer and facilitator, both nationally and internationally, and has taught at Washington University and the University of New Hampshire. Currently, she holds the position of academic director at the Wayne Institute for Advanced Psychotherapy at Bellarmine University. Dr. Gianotti has presented at various professional conferences,
including Division 39 of the APA, Smith College, and the University of Cape Town. Dr. Gianotti is co-author of the book *Listening with Purpose: Entry Points into Shame and Narcissistic Vulnerability*. She lives in North Hampton, NH, with her husband, Stephen.

Jack Danielian, PhD, is a licensed psychologist, supervisor, and dean of the American Institute for Psychoanalysis in New York. He is a training and supervising analyst and on the faculty of the Institute. Dr. Danielian has lectured internationally and nationally on psychoanalytic issues, intercultural communication, and intergenerational effects of genocide. He is the author of numerous professional publications, including co-author of the book *Listening with Purpose: Entry Points into Shame and Narcissistic Vulnerability*. Dr. Danielian is currently training practitioners in Guangzhou, China, and at The Wayne Institute for Advanced Psychotherapy at Bellarmine University. He and his wife live in Potomac, MD.

If you wish to contact Patricia Gianotti or Jack Danielian, they can be reached through their website, www.treatingnarcissism.com.

Index

Page numbers in *italic* indicate figures and tables.